LEFTOVER LUTEFISK:
More Stories from The Lutefisk Ghetto

by
Art Lee

Cover and Illustrations
by
Dee Anne Najjar

published by

Adventure Publications
P.O. Box 269
Cambridge, Minnesota 55008

LEFTOVER LUTEFISK:
More Stories From
The Lutefisk Ghetto

Copyright, 1984
by
Adventure Publications
Cambridge, Minnesota 55008

First Printing, 1984

Second Printing, 1984

Third Printing, 1985

Fourth Printing, 1986

Fifth Printing, 1987

Sixth Printing, 1988

Printed in the United States of America

ISBN 0-934860-32-7

DEDICATION

To All Those Unheralded But Welcomed
SCANDINAVIANS-IN-AMERICA
—Some 2.5 Million Emigrants—
Who Eventually and Essentially Said
It All In A One-Line-Summation Of
Their New Land:

"Vi Har Det Godt I Amerika."
(We Have It Good In America)

. . .We Are Your Children—
And Your Children's Children
And We Thank You For Our Heritage.
—Art Lee

AID (?) DEFINITIONS FOR THE CURIOUS,
IF UNTUTORED. . .

LUTEFISK: A uniquely prepared fish eaten by Scandinavians in general and Norwegians in particular; from the Norwegian words *lute* (meaning to wash in a lye and water solution) and *fisk* (fish). Before the days of refrigeration, fish was often preserved by drying it in the sun, and after it was stored for any length of time, the fish became very hard. At one time lye-water was used to loosen (or soften) the hard fish; and after the fish became soft—and the lye carefully washed off—it would go into boiling water and come out ready to be eaten, usually with melted butter poured over the fish. Lutefisk is served by Scandinavian-Americans primarily at Christmas time nowadays.

GHETTO: As used in this book, the appropriate definition would be: ". . .an isolated or segregated group . . .a section in which members of a distinct cultural group live." **Webster's Third New International Dictionary**

UFF DA: A very common idiomatic expression associated with all Norwegians. The brief phrase generally connotes an element of surprise and/or displeasure, but it is used regularly as an almost conditioned-reflex reaction to such things as: the weather, good/bad news, pondering great thoughts (as in "Uff da, lemme t'ink 'bout dat"), the neighbors' dogs, food on the table, Aunt Minnie's knitting, and other such appropriate times and places where the phrase just comes out so natural.

EVERYTHING YOU ALWAYS WANTED TO KNOW
ABOUT NORWEGIANS BUT WERE AFRAID TO HAVE
CONFIRMED.

"Did you hear that they kept the Knutson kid after school
because he couldn't find the Ozarks."
"Good. Dat'll teach 'im to remember where he put things."

Publisher's Note:

The success of the first publication of **The Lutefisk Ghetto** in 1978 came as a happy surprise to both the author and the publisher. The book had been written essentially for the students in the author's freshmen history classes. He hoped to inform students about life in a small Wisconsin town at the end of World War II as well as to tell them as pleasantly and painlessly as possible about the impact of the war on Americans. He also hoped to educate students about a particular ethnic group who had been Americanized by that time but who were still holding on to some cultural old-world flavors. All of these goals were attained, and the interest in the book spread far beyond the classroom. By 1983 the book was in its sixth printing, with over 13,000 copies sold.

When the editor of the **Red River Valley Heritage Press** out of Fargo-Moorhead found out about the book, he contacted Art Lee and persuaded him to write a monthly column for his regional newspaper, the column to be called appropriately "From the Lutefisk Ghetto." This section of the **Press** became an immediate hit with the readers as reader-surveys showed it to be the most read portion of the newspaper. Many of the columns were reprinted in the **Minneapolis Star-Tribune** as well as several other publications ranging from the **Trail County Tribune** of Mayville, North Dakota, and the **Iola Herald** of Iola, Wisconsin, to **Vinland** in Evanston, Illinois.

Lee's second book on Scandinavians in America, **Leftover Lutefisk: More Stories From The Lutefisk Ghetto**, is a result of bringing his monthly columns all together under one cover. Although the columns may not have originally been published in the order in which they appear in this book, it was thought useful to group them by seasons, hence the sections Summer, Fall, Winter, and Spring. So enjoy reading what might be called: "Everything You Wanted to Know About Norwegians. . . But Were Afraid to Have Confirmed."

. . .REGARDING READER RESPONSE AND THE QUESTION: *"Where is this 'Lutefisk Ghetto' anyway?"*

The most common response from readers of the first *Lutefisk Ghetto* was for them to write to the author or publisher and say in effect: What the book really described was my hometown, too.

It is evident from both letters and comments that not only were there dozens if not hundreds of similar Scandinavian communities throughout the Middle West, but also reader responses indicate that these towns and townspeople are still out there; there are plenty of 'Lutefisk Ghettoes' today.

The primary geographical area discussed by the author in both books, of course, is the locale around Scandinavia, Wisconsin. Several of his columns, however, are based on his experiences while living in Iowa and North Dakota as well as his present address at Bemidji, Minnesota. Yet judging from the letters he received, he realized that *The Lutefisk Ghetto* was essentially based on Scandinavia, U.S.A.

Whatever or wherever the towns, past or present, the author apparently touched a common nerve for many readers. Obviously there was and is a commonality for citizens who either grew up or still live in small rural towns.

In yet another related matter, even the ethnic factor seemed interchangeable as many people wrote to comment how their town was "just like" this Norwegian community, except that in their case the dominant ethnic group was Swedish—or Danish, or Finnish, or German, or French, or Irish—but other than for the nationality substitution, their towns were "just the same." It appears that Ethnic America is very much alive and well.

CONTENTS

Explaining a Curious Norwegian custom...

Since Sven Forkbeard's dragon ship
Didst cross the Poison Sea,
The Norseman has been noted for
His wild ferocity.

He plundered all the British Isles
And all their women bedded,
And left behind a legacy
Of Irishmen red-headed.

From Norway to west, to Vinland,
And Eastward, past Murmansk,
Went the plundering hoary hordes
Of Norsk, and Svensk and Dansk.

At home, they played with axes;
They swilled strong drink from bowls;
And instead of cuddly teddy bears,
They gave their kids stuffed trolls.

Their thunder was Thor's hammer
As it roared across the sea,
Each day brought Götterdämmerung
And flights of Valkyrie.

The Vikings were the fiercest guys
What ever trod the Earth,
And they passed their fearsome heritage
Along their lines of birth.

But meanness isn't in their genes,
And it isn't in their blood
I think it comes, quite naturally,
From Scandinavian food.

If man is only what he eats,
Then, I have found the reason
For Svensk and Norsk eat Lutefisk
Whenever it's in season.

They salt and air-dry Cod Fish
Till it's like a two-by-four
Then they soak the fish in lye a week,
Then rinse, and soak some more.

The smell of soaking Lutefisk,
As it wafts across the fjord,
Can ruin TV reception and
Pop knotholes from a board.

But Norsemen love their Lutefisk;
And they can hardly wait,
To take it from the lye barrel
And put it on their plate.

Some even eat it long before
The lye has all been rinsed,
And that is why the Norseman
Has been meaner ever since.

In truth it takes a true Norseman,
To eat a cod so soaked;
For lesser men have held their nose
And eaten it, and croaked.

So please, don't blame the Norseman
For being such a risk;
It's not his father's heritage;
It's his mother's Lutefisk.

"Some even eat it long before
"The lye has all been rinsed,
"And that is why the Norseman
"Has been meaner ever since."

Summer is the hardest time for Norwegians. You have to ride around with all of the windows up so that the neighbors will think that you have air conditioning.

SUMMER

A Saturday Night in August

Main street is filled with parked cars, many of which were brought and left there in the afternoon so that there will be no chance of the owners missing the evening's Great Parade. (ca. 1950)

The Parade is composed only of people passing by on the sidewalk in front of the parked cars. Everyone but everyone must walk up and down the sidewalks on both sides of the streets at least once on a summer Saturday night. It's expected. Otherwise how else will people know who is and who is not in town?

In the parked cars the windows are sure to be open if there is a car radio to play. To use the radio loudly is clear evidence to the sidewalk sidlers of money and status. After all, just anyone can't afford a radio in his car; it's too much of a luxury.

Up on the sidewalks the age groups are gathering. Two high school boys, wearing their heavy letter-sweaters—with their shiny pins and chevrons and stripes denoting local herodom—despite the hot night, congregate on one main corner so as not to miss any girls who walk by.

Soon two high school girls stroll past the boys, walking slowly enough to be properly seen and fast enough so as not to appear too easy to pick-up. One girl is very pretty, the other plain and unattractive.

"There's Belva Hanson and Oogus Hovdahl," whispers one boy. (Her real name is Gladyce but she's usually called Oogus, short for Ugly.) "How come girls always pair up, and how come one is always such a dish and the other one such a dog?" asks the puzzled boy to his friend who only replies, "Beats me." The friend turns to watch classmate Sigurd Olson go by yet again up and down main street in his 1928 Model A, the squirrel-tail swinging from the aerial, the enlarged rubber dice cubes swaying back and forth from the rear-view mirror.

Sigurd spies Belva, then shoves up the spark lever and switches the ignition key off and on quickly, producing the loud backfire—BANG!—that he intended. That burst of noise is followed by the distinctive sound of a Model A horn—"OOOoooOOO-Gah"—but Belva turns away. "That Sig Olson can be such a jerk sometimes," says Belva, who nevertheless appreciates attention.

"I think he's cute!" says Oogus, her companion. "Gol-lee, whata hunk!"

"C'mon, let's hurry and meet him, but when we get up to where our moms are, we'll slow down and pretend we're looking at the stuff in the dry-goods window," says Belva.

Just up the street stand the girls' farm mothers, both of whom are done trading at the stores. The ladies come to town to socialize and "to trade," trading, in a literal sense, their eggs and butter and even live chickens for groceries.

"Whatcha got in dat big bag, den?" asks Emma, teasingly, knowing well that each has essentially the same groceries. "Ay got only a ten-pound bag uf Gold Medal flour diss time, 'causs *je er sa sint paa dem*(I am so angry with them). Da bread hardly raised t'ree inches in da last batch. Lewked like teeny t'ings some Roosian lady make."

"Yeah-da, den. Dey don' make flour like dey used to," agrees Gudren. " 'Course could be da yeast, tew. Anyvay, ay alvays buy Robin Hood. My Palmer he sess dat's da best." "Yah?" "Yah."

Both look up when they hear the Model-A backfiring. "Yeepers! Sounds yust like da For't of July," exclaims Emma, who then spies the culprit. "Fee-da, scum, it's dat Olson *gutt*(boy) showin' off. Myrna Hoyard—and she knowss all da dirt—tell me dat hiss fodder hass hiss hands full vit dat jung vippersnapper." "Yah?" "Yah."

"Le's hope to heffen dat our girlses neffer git mixed up with HIM!"

"Vell, iff effer Ay sees dat girl-a-mine gittin'in dat car, dere'll be VAR!"

Across the street from the women-folk stand their husbands, Palmer and Walter, who have also heard the loud backfiring.

"Hey dere, den. Did yew hear dat? Ay t'ink dat da constable oughta haff a little talk vit dat Olson kid. He acts like hees got haff a shine on. A smart-aleck, if yew ask me, den."

"Vorse den dat, " replies Walter. "Dey say he ain't no gewd on da farm. Dey say all he vants to do iss drive da tractor. Von't do no barn vork. A regular fancy-pants, aye t'ink." "Yah?" "Yah."

"Vell, den, hver vere ve? O yeah, how vuss dat oat crop on da back forty? T'ick?"

"T'in. T'irty bushels to da acre uf oats—and tew bushels uf t'istles, tew."

"Yah-da, da t'istle harvest iss gewd diss year," replies Palmer with a grin. "Uff da, here come dat Olson kid back up da street again, and. . . HERRE GUD! (Holy God) Dere he shot off anudder vun!"

"He gonna blow dat dang muffler into a t'ousand pieces! Aye gotta mind to tell hiss Pa 'bout dat li'l **drit-saek.**"

"Don't do no gewd. Hiss folks spoil him rotten. Iff he vuss my kid, Ayd'a laid a razor-strop on hiss boomers long ago."

"Vell, if he vuss mine, Ayd'a drowned him in da horse tank long ago."

"Ve better hope dat dose young ladies of ours neffer take up vit da likes av dat goof."

"**Akkurat** (Exactly). But dey're smart 'nuff to figger out vhat hee's after. If not, ay gonna lock my girl up in da shicken coop and t'row 'vay da key."

The Model A turns the corner on the north end of main street and stops, timing the turn with the arrival of Belva and Oogus. "Hey there" hollers the driver to Belva. "Wanna go for a spin?"

"Not unless Gladyce goes with."

Hesitation. Then, "Sure, c'mon 'long. Git in the back seat, Oogus, but don't sit down hard and break my jar. I sneaked a quart of grape wine from the crock in the cellar before vamoosin' to town."

"Hurry, Sig. We gotta be back in an hour. Let's cut out before our folks see us," says an excited and half-scared Belva.

"Let's all go to the lake and go swimmin!" says Oogus, who then stops, then adds, "'Cept we forgot our swimsuits."

"Great idea!" exclaims Sig. "We'll drink the wine on the way and by the time we get there we won't worry 'bout no swim suits."

"Well, maybe," says Belva.

"Sounds like fun to me!" says Oogus, "but we dasn't never let our folks know."

"Naw, they'll never find out," says Sig. "And besides, old people never care what young people do anyway."

The Thrill of Threshing

Down the twisting, narrow and graveled driveway came a clattering parade of wagons and tractors, horses and men. Leading the line of wagons and hay-rigs was a massive Oliver tractor pulling a more massive J.I. Case threshing machine, its heavy iron wheels crushing the limestone pebbles that lay in its way.

The aging thresher was owned together by all the farmers along both sides of Bestul creek. Once a year the creaking Case was hauled out from a machine shed and into the daylight for two weeks, a fortnight of constant motion as it swallowed and spewed out the million bundles of shocked oats fed into its mincing maw by the Moe brothers, two carefully chosen men who would properly pitch—not too fast, not too slow—all the shocked grain that grew on both sides of Bestul creek.

Soon the thresher was skillfully pushed and prodded between the stacks, and the wheels were blocked by rocks and wood chunks so it would not budge either direction. The fat black pulley belt was attached from the belly of the thresher to the pulley wheel on the tractor, and then the tractor backed up slowly, carefully, the belt tightening between the two ancient machines at just the right tension for Truls Arstad to yell: "Stop! Das it! Now get 'er in gear an' let 'er rip!"

The once sagging Oliver seemed to spring alive, roaring loudly; the greasy black conveyor belt squeaked and grunted and groaned as little by little the belt turned slowly, then faster and faster, speeding up to the point when suddenly the thresher came alive, too, and it roared back at the tractor.

"Yah-da, den; she's ready!" hollered Truls over the pounding noise. "T'row dose bundles, Moe boyss! An' let's git diss show on da vroad." And like metronomes, the Moe brothers moved their three-tined pitch forks in a constant fluid motion that seemed to find one shock of grain in the air at all times.

A long, fat pipe from the thresher stuck way out from the end of the machine and already straw and dirt and chaff were flying out of its mouth. Underneath stood Hans Skogsbakken, oblivious to the dirty showering from the pipe. He was stomping and stamping down some tied-together gunny sacks that would make a kind of floor for the strawpile that was just starting.

It was Hans Skogsbakken's day, his turn—and he thanked the Lord it was only one day he had to do it—to spend the day in the straw stack. Within two hours he would be so covered with dirt and chaff that he'd look like an African; by the end of the day the layers would be measured in inches. "Hoohoo! Lewk at Hans! Maybe he's da Boogie-man!" laughed the Moe boys.

Out in the field rolled the empty hay wagons, a few pulled by tractors but most pulled by horses, and one rig was powered by a pair of black mules. The two forty-acre oat fields were speckled with neatly stacked shocks of grain, each looking like a little pup-tent, each field like an Army bivouac.

The Moe boys moved in synchronized motion, the bundles never stopping in their flight towards the growling mincing-machine. Below them strong shoulders moved steadily with their sacks of grain; nimble fingers kept filling more sacks tied quickly with a miller's knot, the filled bags set along the vibrating thresher.

Hans Skogsbakken now stood high off the ground and was

almost invisible as he shaped and rounded the strawstack amid the black clouds of chaff and straw that pounded and poured endlessly from the eight inch chute above him.

Hei du (Hey you!) yelled Jim Bestful to the Moe boys. "Dinner time!" **Kom og spis!** (Come and eat!) Orvis Moe, heretofore never halting his motion, stopped long enough to grab a leather strap and pull out an Ingraham pocket watch from in his overalls. "Yah-da, den; ve stoop."

Hand signals went to Truls on the tractor; fingers began pushing throttles and pulling levers. In thirty seconds the deafening roar had turned to total silence. Empty hay wagons were strung out on the path to the fields, the horses unhitched, the bridles replaced with halters, and the teams led one by one to the round trough of water where they drank and drank until the owners decided the moment when enough was enough.

Outside the summer-kitchen the men lined up before the hand pump. With complete understanding, the men let Hans Skogsbakken move to the front of the line but not without some good-natured commenting:

"**Fie scum**! And ay tought Trolls vere ugly!"

"**Nei, men har du sett slik**? (No, but have you seen such a thing?) An' ve vere tol' dat da devil vass bad-lookin'."

Around the huge oak table, with every extra leaf inserted to achieve maximum length, sat high straight-back chairs with spindle legs. The men moved in quickly without hesitating after the first **vaer saa god** (come and eat).

Deep dishes with steaming boiled potatoes moved quickly from one set of rough hands to another; heavy platters of well-done roast beef followed at the same speed. Then came piles of piping hot green beans; then biscuits and jelly and jam and beet pickles and over the heaped plates of food rolled thick, blistering-hot brown gravy.

"Haff anudder helpin', den," said the Missus who was up as early as her husband to insure the meal being ready on time.

"Nei takk (no thanks). T'ree helpin's iss enuff; gotta safe some vroom for da mince-meat pie."

The mountainous meal finished, men slowly sagged away

"On a small hillside next to the barn sat a little tow-headed boy who had been there since dawn. . . . 'Threshing day was magnificent.' "

> *"Then came piles of piping hot green beans; then biscuits and jelly and jam and beet pickles and over the heaped plates of food rolled thick, blistering-hot brown gravy."*

from their chairs. Some meandered out on the front lawn and immediately lay down on the grass. Several men sat in the shade next to the house, resting their backs against the cool rock foundation, and there they hauled out stumpy pipes and Prince Albert tobacco cans and silently puffed away.

"Y'know?" said Norman Olson. "Dese tings could end soon. Dey sell more of dose combines effrey year."

"Nei, da," answered Kjitel Kjendalen. "Combines vaste tew much oats. T'reshin' iss da best."

"Akkarat (Exactly). Uff da, aye see tiss time to git back to vork. Vork iss da curse of da drinkin' man."

★ ★ ★ ★

On a small hillside next to the barn sat a little towheaded boy who had been there since dawn. He was close enough to see everything, and far enough to be out of everybody's way. What he saw and heard and smelled and touched was to him all so wonderful. Threshing day was magnificent! The memories would be permanently fixed in his mind, and today I remember it all as well as if it were only yesterday.

The Weekly Summer Band Concerts

There has been a big, fancy word around the country lately called "ethnicity." The term is supposed to suggest a reawakened interest in one's foreign or semi-foreign background—language, habits, attitudes, and the like—as though one could ever forget them.

Who could forget inadvertently hearing "ethnicity," for

example, while sitting in the back seat of a 1939 Ford parked on Main Street on a Saturday night just as Aunt Tilla spies her cousin Aleda outside.

The window gets rolled down lickety-split, and the conversation begins:

"Vell, hey dere, den. Are yew in town, tew?"

"Yah-shooer, Ay gass so."

"Tiss nice out, den."

"Oh yah, but it vuss hot tew-day. Vere is yur Telford?"

"Ay tank he's in Aasen's Dry Goods to git some new bibs."

Both Aunt Tilla and cousin Aleda knew that Uncle Telford was in the pool hall drinking beer, the only safe refuge in town where no self-respecting woman would go and retrieve him.

"Why don't you come in and sit a little?"

"Vell, yust a little," said Aleda.

"Den vee can wiss-it."

"Yah-dah. Uff da, but ay vish dat band not play so loud, den, cause ay can't hear yew."

"Vell, Telford's li'l neffer—Sonja's youngest boy—plays da tuba, and ve're sposed to lissen for him. But let's shut da vindow up."

Neither person would have missed a Saturday night in town, regardless if there was a band concert. The concert was incidental; it was the "wissiting" that was all important.

"Yeepers! Loo-ook at dem two! He iss patting her on her boomers!"

"The concert was incidental; it was the 'wissiting' that was all important."

"Hoo hoo! Dey lewk like tew dogs in heat. Fee-da."

"Yah, and she iss always in shurch on Sundays!"

"Vell, she shewd lissen to dat sermon on 'dultery' 'for she git peegee."

"Yah, you can say dat again."

"Oh! Dere's Agnes Lovik. Yeepers! But iss she fat!"

"Yah-dah. Shees t'ree ax-handles across da beam iff she iss an inch."

"Maybe she swallowed anudder vatermelon seed. She turned Cat-lic hven she got married, and yew know how dey are!"

"Dat's ta-rew. Cat-lic ladies iss full of little babies. Uff da."

(The reference to watermelon seeds was a quickly chosen euphemism aimed at the callow lad in the back seat so that young ears would never hear either of two no-no words, pregnant and sex. Yet the reference to Catholic fecundity seemed a bit too much, even then.)

"Vell, den, how duss your Artur like his nee-ew job in da sheese-factory?" asked Aunt Tilla.

"Oh hoot-ma-toot! But he qvit da first day!"

"Huh? Wa hoppen, den? Iss dat tarew?"

"Yah. Yah. Da bossman sess to Artur dat he can't chew snoose and make sheese at da same time."

"Smart feller, dat Artur. No big Swede kin tell him what tew do."

At this point Uncle Telford came up to the car, stuck his head in the window, giving off a strong aroma of Blatz's finest beer. "Hey dere, Aleda. Are yew in town tew?"

But Aunt Tilla interrupted any reply. "Fee-Scum! Yew stink like a brewree! Ish da!"

Telford's timing was perfect. On the bandstand the members were standing up, reaching for their horn cases, and putting their music away in folders. Car horns all along the street began to honk a two-minute thank-you for the performance to which few had listened very carefully, if at all.

"Vell, it iss dat time again tew go home." said Telford.

"Ay gass so," said Aleda, and then to Tilla: "Iss yew done wit yer shopping?"

"Ay tank so."

"Vell, Ay gotta git some pickled herring," said Aleda as she crawled out of the car, "and den find my hussband. Ay vunder hvere he is. Vell, *god nat* (good night.)"

"Yah. *God nat*. Vee skal see you in shurch in da morn."

The cars streamed down main street and began fanning out as they hit the four corners south of town. They would reassemble the next Saturday night on main street hours ahead of the starting time of the band concert, there to get a good seat, there to watch the world go by through the windshields, and there to wiss-it.

"Ethnicity" they call it now; we just called it home.

Every Day Thanksgiving in America

The men gathered daily on the chairs in front of Robert Hanson's Hardware Store. They had other places to assemble, of course—maybe sitting on the concrete ledges on the front of Karl Jorgen's Grocery, or maybe relaxing on the bench and nail kegs by Gustav Jole's Barbershop— but usually the Hardware Store location became the proper forum, the accepted stage for the men to discuss all topics and issues of the day.

Almost all of the men were retired farmers. A few of them had emigrated from Sweden, while the rest were the children of emigrants from Denmark, and thus everyone felt close to the old country.

In their daily sessions they talked and talked, chewed snoose or Summertime or Union Leader tobacco, smoked MANGE pipefuls of Prince Albert or Sir Walter Raleigh TOBAK; they spat, coughed, wheezed, laughed, grunted, swore mildly—and carried on a continuous dialog.

Their conversations were generally convivial, but on occasion the men did get their danders up when the topic was a lively one, as, for example, comparing the merits of Norway over America.

The issue of the United States versus The Old Country regularly generated much heat but not too much light, like this one day when Tobias Fjelstul set the tone for a debate by declaring with great firmness: 'Vi har det godt i Amerika" (We have it good in America).

"Yah," echoed a chorus of agreement. "Akkurat" (exactly), said one voice; "you betcher-bewts," said another.

"The Hardware Store location became the proper forum for the men to discuss all topics and issues of the day."

But Ivar Tollefsrud was not completely convinced by one simple declaration. "Hah!" he snorted in disgust, "Tiss a lot more purdee (pretty) in Norway. Diss place," he continued with a sweep of his arm and in a wide motion suggesting disparagement, "diss place iss nuttin' to look at. Not like HOME."

"Oh yah?" replied Elmo Erickson, his own arm sweeping in an arc, "Ay tink it lewks yust like MY home Terr-tory. Tiss wery purdee."

"Yah-da, den," replied Ivar, with a hint of sarcasm, "but home for yew vuss dat farmin' district at Toten, nort av Oslo. Dat ain't da ta-rew Norvay. An' 'sides," he added with disdain, "dose Toten folk neffer did learn to talk vright."

"ISS DAT SO!" thundered Elmo, his anger rising quickly. "Whatcha mean 'not talk right' Yew gice talk goofy, ay tink; yew gice talk Norsk like dere's a hot potato stuck in da t'roat. Sound vorse den a bunch av Danes! Now poot dat in yur pipe an' smoke it."

"We can't help where we come from, and so naturally we talk different dialects, but that's nothin' to git so all fired up about. Uff da."

"Now hold your horses!" interjected Hans Rasmusson, always the peacemaker when tempers flared. "We can't help where we come from, and so naturally we talk different dialects, but that's nothin' to git so all fired up about. Uff da."

There followed murmured assents and grunts of agreement. After all, there was no real reason to get so confounded angry. And so peace settled in briefly while they all agreed that the weather sure had been dry for a long spell. But Ivar couldn't leave a good thing alone:

"Lewk at diss geog-phry 'round here, den. Tiss flat azz a pankaker. Ay tay yew dat ve need mountains for real bee-ew-tee (beauty)! All dose **aaser** (ridges) sout' of town iss ant-hills compared to back home on da Sognfjord," he declared firmly.

Then he stopped and relighted his corncob pipe with a farmers-stick, swiping the match along the thigh of his overalls to light it. Let them try to refute THAT last statement.

Ivar had indeed made a valid observation, as noted by some grudging grunts of assent. Mountains were surely beautiful, all right, and the ridgeline of hills around their own town were nothing compared to the Westland of Norway. Everyone seemed to buy the argument except Lars Li.

Lars, once a 19-year-old emigrant from the Laerdahl district at the end of Sognfjord, had had just about enough of Ivar's foolish talk, and Lars' English was better than his Norwegian when it came time to say something he felt so strongly about:

"In Laerdahl we were surrounded on three sides by mountains, and wherever we looked there were waterfalls coming out from dese mountain walls. Yah-sure, it was a beautiful place. And usually da mist and fog hung all morning on da rims of da mountains and filtered da sun's rays coming through, changing da color patterns. Diss scenery was so lovely that it could take your breat' away."

"Dat's hvat ay try'n to tell effreybody!" interrupted Ivar, believing he had found a partner for his side.

"Ivar," said Lars sternly, fixing a hold on him with anguished eyes, "you can't eat beauty."

"Nei (No), but. . ."

"But nothin'! Us eight kids lived in a two-room farm-shack at da bottom of dis mountain. And we hardly ever had enough to eat! We ate nothin' but grøt (porridge), grøt, and more grøt, with every person digging as fast as possible, like pigs, when we dipped our spoons into diss one big bowl in da middle of da table."

"Nei, but. . ."

"But nothin'! Out our only window we could view da most lovely mountain scene one could ever imagine. But you can't eat scenery! The beauty was mocking beauty. We were practically starving!"

"Nei, but. . ."

"Ivar, you know dat to be true, you stubborn Norwegian.

Compared to what most of us had in da old country, every day in America has been like Thanksgiving Day. Ivar, admit it, *vi har det godt i Amerika!*"

Ivar heaved a big sigh, then nodded his head both in agreement and concession of defeat. "Yah, dass vright. Tiss Ta-rue. An' hvat yew say sess it all: *Vi har det godt i Amerika.* Now, den, le's talk 'bout diss terr-ble dry vetter ve're haffin. . ."

Thawing A Cold Norwegian

She sat alone in the back seat of Pa's old Hudson, her bulging homemade purse on her one side, a large shoebox—filled with sandwiches, pickles, and apples—on the other side. The latter would provide both her lunch and supper on the long bus ride to Iowa.

The shoebox had been stuffed full by her mother, the graying, pug-haired lady who now sat in the front seat and who was busy chattering to the bored-looking driver, her father. Then the mother turned around to add:

"Vell, den, it seems to me dat yew could git a teachin' yob at home. Ve got schools in dis state tew, y'know. But *nei* (no), yew go far avay, My my my my my."

The girl was leaving home and the farm, planning never to return except for maybe a couple of days' visiting. Now she had her brand new two-year teaching certificate from the state teachers college; now she could strike out on her own; now she could made the break and gain independence. And yet she dreaded the long bus ride and all the uncertainties and doubts, especially about her father.

Despite all the clucking and the "my mys," she knew her mother would understand, that Ma would let go, that she loved her daughter fervently and told her so often.

But what about Pa? Did he understand? Would he let her go? Did Pa love her? She didn't know the answers to any of these things for the simple reason that Pa never said what he knew or how he felt. Pa never said anything.

"The shoebox had been stuffed full by her mother. . . . 'Ve got schools in dis state tew, y'know.' "

Here she was, the last child, the final kid to leave the homeplace. Didn't Pa care about her at all? Didn't he ever show emotion? What's wrong with these Norwegians? Haven't they got any feelings at all?

She had watched her Pa as her oldest brother marched off to the war, and Pa never as much said a warm goodbye, let alone give him a hug. There was only that cold and formal handshake, no different than the one he gave the minister every Sunday morning at 11 a.m.

"She remembered the time when he picked up the end of the car when the jack slipped and held it up 'til her brother got the tire on."

Her father's apparent lack of feelings bothered her greatly, and she had once complained to her mother about it, to no avail, Ma unable to explain except to say:

"Heess a gewd man. He yust dussn't much say how he feels. But he alvays tewk gewd care of hiss family, den. He iss strong, y'know."

Pa was strong, all right, that she knew. He was the strongest man she'd ever seen! She remembered the time when he picked up the end of the car when the jack slipped and held it up til her brother got the tire on. She'd seen him grab two big young farm-hands at a wedding dance who were about ready to fight. Pa grabbed one under each arm and held them so tight that he squeezed the breath out of both of them, and he let go only when they gasped out their promise to behave themselves.

And once when she got off the school bus and was walking down the driveway, she looked up and witnessed an unbeliev-able scene. Pa was out plowing with a single plow pulled by Molly, their draft horse, when a car stopped and a man got out and asked Pa for directions to the Dahlen place. Pa picked up the plow and pointed it in the direction of the Dahlens, then gently put the plow back in the furrow and continued what he was doing before the interruption.

Now her Pa sat in front of her, this massive man with the impassive face. His full, droopy, walrus moustache needed trimming, and this Ma would do as she did every Sunday morning before church. She watched his pale blue eyes in the rearview mirror and she could not see one hint of feeling in them, not one sign of affection, not one glint that he would miss his only daughter.

But she would miss him. She would miss his quiet dignity, this man who would noisily slurp his hot coffee from a saucer but who would not remove his suitcoat nor loosen his tie on the hottest day in church because it would not look right. She would miss his honesty, this man who ate peas with a knife but who returned a check to the co-op because they had overpaid him by three dollars. She would miss his generosity, this man who chewed snoose and who never removed the chaw all day even at meal times, but this same man who picked blueberries after chores every night and sold them until there was enough money to pay for her college tuition. It would be a long ride to Iowa.

When they reached the four corners, where the county road met the state highway, the Hudson pulled off the gravel and stopped in the parking lot next to Haugen's General Store. Anyone who wanted to ride the bus stood out in front of the store by the highway and hailed the bus driver to stop.

While Pa went to get the suitcases from the trunk, Ma chattered and frittered: "Dat fodder of yurs iss da slowest da-river in diss 'hole vide vorld. Dat buss vill be here inny moment," and sure enough, when they turned and looked, they could both see and hear this aging machine a half mile away. The ride to Iowa looked longer all the time.

"Yah-da, den, dis iss it," said Ma. "Tiss gewdbye to our baby," and with that line Ma's eyes began to well up. Mother and daughter embraced warmly, all the time the mother giving last minute advice: "Now don' let inny jung whipper-snapper giff yew candy or treats on da bus. Dose gice iss dainch-rus!"

Pa stood off to the side. He had not said a word the whole trip and wasn't planning to start now. With both hands in the pockets of his bib overalls, he poked at the gravel with his foot and looked down at the ground.

The daughter looked at him and then said to herself, Ah, why not? With that she walked quickly over to her father, stood on her tip-toes, put both arms around his neck and hugged him as absolutely hard as she could as she said, "Pa, I love you."

Then came her miracle. Pa's huge arms then encircled her and he squeezed her so hard that she thought every rib would crack. For a moment it was the most wonderful pain she had ever experienced. Then came the best of all, some accented words whispered very quietly and directed to the top of her head: "Ay luff yew, tew."

The bus ride to Iowa wasn't so bad after all.

The Funeral's Over, Pass the Pickles

The car pulled hurriedly into the town and the driver, quickly noting the small size of the community, decided he would not have to take time to stop and ask directions to the church. He'd find it easily and make it to the funeral on time.

There was only one church in town, the Lutheran Church, a charming-looking, dark-brown brick structure standing on the end of Main Street, just where the main highway turned right leading out of town to yet another lutefisk ghetto four miles away.

It was coincidental that this stranger from the city was there at all that day. He had been vacationing in the area and by accident happened to pick up the local county newspaper, and he spotted the obituary of a man he had once known well. The two of them had worked side by side on an assembly-line back during the Second World War.

Although going to funerals was not his idea of being on vacation, the stranger felt both a tinge of obligation as well as curiosity to find out what small-town funerals up north were like.

★ ★ ★ ★ ★

The church's parking lot was almost filled as he pulled into the driveway, and this made the stranger conclude that the deceased must have been well known and well liked. After all, isn't a funeral the true test of one's popularity?

Inside the church the first thing he noticed—and thought it peculiar—was the strong smell of food and coffee coming up from the basement.

Before he could figure out the reason for the food odors, the service started, and this led to a few more eye-openers for him. He didn't understand why the entire family of the deceased, a few sobbing almost uncontrollably, had to be marched right up to the front row for the whole world to see. Was this some kind of show? he wondered.

Nor did he like the idea of the casket being wheeled up the middle aisle, then opened up when it arrived at the front of the pulpit. But the real jolt came next—causing him to wince—when the whole congregation got up row by row to file by the open casket to gaze down at the remains.

The actual service itself, however, was agreeable to the stranger. The Bible verses chosen were supportive, the hymns selected were uplifting even if few people opened their mouths to sing; and the pastor's message had well-chosen, thoughtful words that were comforting for the family and for the other people listening so quietly, showing no emotions.

So the stranger concluded that all in all it was a meaningful funeral, with all there showing proper decorum and solemnity in paying final respects to the deceased and his family. The taboo-topic of death was dealt with in a manner that left all in attendance with a message of courage and hope. Nice funerals, up north.

Then at the very end of the service, the pastor changed both his manner and the tone of his voice when he made the announcement that all there were invited on behalf of the family—and through the help of the Ladies Aid—to have "a little lunch" downstairs immediately afterwards.

This one line of the pastor's did more to stir the congregation than anything he had said the past forty-five minutes. People in the pews began to smile openly; others nodded and murmured approval of what they heard. A couple almost seemed to sniff the air in anticipation, the smell of the coffee getting stronger up in the church proper.

The stranger, too, decided to get "a little lunch," as much as anything to find out just what was going on downstairs. And what was going on downstairs was to shock him even more. The funeral above had given way to a party below. Laughing, convivial people were shaking hands and trading stories and discussing the weather in what was definitely a happy, social atmosphere.

Surprises continued when he looked at the food on the tables. "A little lunch" was more like a full dinner! Platters of meats and cheeses were on both ends, and in between were more plates of open-faced sandwiches while interspersed between were jello bowls and hot-dishes. In the few places left open he could see shrimp salad, beet salad, pea salad, and fish salad. And as he looked in amazement, the food was disappearing amazingly fast amid loud conversations.

The stranger tried to listen to the words but it was difficult because of the general noise that sounded like a riot in a parrot-house. But here and there a few lines came through:

"Diss noodle-dish iss better den yew make, Maw."

"Hows's da fishin', den?"

"Ay t'ink ve need rain bad, den. Da pastures iss dry asz a bone."

And so it went. The stranger was first taken back but then figured he should not be a wet blanket and amid all this gaiety, so he sat down beside a couple whose English didn't sound so foreign and asked:

"Did you know the deceased well?" and his new-found eating-partner replied: "Nope. Not really. In fact I didn't know him at all, but our neighbors knew him and they were going to the funeral and we didn't have nuthin' to do, so we decided to go, too. We kinda like funerals."

"Oh, well. . .yes, of course." It was time to change the subject. "What's this stuff on this plate? It looks like cardboard backing material."

"That's flatbread! Yeepers, but that's a good one. Didn't even know **flatbrød!** Hoo hoo hoo!"

The stranger smiled meekly, then excused himself and found another chair in the very opposite corner. Once again he tried conversation with a new neighbor: "Were you a friend of the deceased?"

"The who?"

"Uh, the man who died. Y'know. . .the funeral?"

"Met him once. Nice guy. Pass the pickles."

"Sure. Sure. By the way, what are the waitresses putting on the tables now?"

"Lemme see. Yup, you've got your choice of **fystekake, eplekake, krumkake, or epletoska.**"

"Excuse me, but I don't understand---."

"Cakes!"

"Oh yes, of course."

"The funeral for my cousin Torben last month was better than this. Not only did they serve creamy layer cakes but hot-dogs in lefse, too. Boy-o-boy, but ve sure ate good at that funeral!"

The stranger got up to leave and as he walked outside towards the parking lot, he was unsure if the people up north had the right idea or not about funerals. Then again that egg salad sandwich and the cheez-whiz on rye bread sure tasted good.

When The 'Moon' Comes Over The Ball Field

Time was when summer Sunday afternoon baseball was the biggest thing around for both small and large communities in the Upper Midwest.

Whatever the size of the town—ten or ten thousand—the summer ball team provided entertainment for large numbers of area citizens who loved and supported their local teams. Town baseball was once a way of life.

Before television, before two cars in every garage, before trips to the lake cottage for the weekend, people came out in large numbers to root for the locals at the town ballpark. Thrills for fans for fifty cents.

Before Americanization and/or "integration," every lutefisk ghetto—and sauerkraut ghetto and/or moika or pasta or potica or croissants or kielbasa ghetto—had a town baseball team. A team went with the territory.

Some of the towns with ballclubs were legally not even towns, not even incorporated villages. A store and a gas station at some four-corners was often enough designation of a locale to host and produce a squad from the surrounding rural area. No matter how small a community, however, the enthusiasm for the local products was there. And besides, what else was there to do on a Sunday afternoon?

The quality of the ball players themselves, of course, varied widely, not only from team to team but for the same team from game to game. On some Sundays players couldn't beat a pick-up bunch of Campfire Girls, while on other weekends they played like big league professionals. This unevenness made for interesting contests and plays. Hence every flyball lofted high and lazily into the outfield gave spectators the thrill of anticipation as to whether the ball would be caught or whether it would come down and hit the player on the head.

Amateur baseball was contradictory in other ways, too, in that it was both serious and fun. Certainly won-loss records built community pride—or village embarrassment. Sometimes the game got so serious that the definition of the term "amateur" was compromised because some special players were picking up clandestine bucks under the table for playing these "games for fun." Also frequent betting on games led to more bucks being exchanged, with bets on some important games approaching four figures. And sometimes "games" turned so hostile that uniformed persons had to be escorted out of town with police protection. There is no wrath like that of a fan who knows the umpire is blind.

But sandlot baseball was fun, too, and sometimes funny, depending on the particular players and managers. On occasion the fun and the seriousness was mixed up and convoluted because what the manager took to be so serious was what the fans took to be so funny.

A case in point was the manager of our town team, one Gordon Trinrud, who essentially took all games seriously, including his coaching part in the contests. But fans found watching the serious Gordon puff and snort and throw tantrums in the coaching box to be often more entertaining than the game itself.

Gordon's Sunday afternoon steady diet of quack grass, his wild gesticulations during some exciting play, his nervous pipe-smoking (twelve lightings to one fill), his hurling of his cap to the ground when disgusted, his uninhibited prancing (called the Gordon One Step) immediately following a victory, were all delights for amused spectators to observe.

An additional frequent flair of Gordon's was for him to look suspiciously at the squad's favorite player and character, the portly Bucky Carr, who might be standing quietly at his third base position doing nothing wrong. Then something inexplicable would motivate Gordon to burst forth at the strangest moment the strangest request: "Geeeee-SUSS, Bucky, DO SOME-THING!"

And this line sent fans into paroxyms of laughter, in part because of the curious timing, in part because they knew the associations of the pair off the playing field. Gordon owned the major tavern in town; Bucky was his chief bartender. At times their close relationship resembled father and son, but on the ball field it was sometimes more like Rocky Marciano versus Sugar Ray Robinson. Yet on and off the field, they made a great pair.

Bucky was a young bachelor of uncommon easy manner with a marvelous personality. Everybody but everybody loved Bucky. Having sampled regularly the products he bestowed on his thirsty customers, Bucky had achieved considerable girth, much of which hung over the front of his belt. At ball games Bucky's "Milwaukee Goiter" produced much comment from baseball fans, to wit: "Hey Bucky, take that basketball out from under your uniform!" And the crowd would laugh while Bucky would just smile.

Bucky was a character partly because he didn't try to be one. It just happened; to him it came so naturally. For example, at least once each game the umpire had to stop the contest at the most inopportune time while Bucky chased his Springer Spaniel around the ball diamond trying to get the dog out of there. The crowds loved it, and loved him.

> *"Bucky was a character partly because he didn't try to be one. It just happened; to him it came so naturally."*

And at least once a game, Bucky in the batter's box would practically jump up and swing at a pitch some four feet over his head, an event which caused fans and Gordon to erupt, but each with a different reaction to Bucky's attempt to swat low-flying blackbirds. (Gordon regretted one eruption. He happened to be sitting in a dugout where the ceiling was five feet high and Gordon was six feet tall. When he leaped up in anger, he was quickly back down again, holding his aching head. Then Bucky laughed.)

Despite his dumpling figure, and despite all the good-natured kidding he got from the sidelines, Bucky was an excellent third baseman who could knock down any batted ball that came near him, and he had a shot-gun arm to first base. And despite his ample girth, he could run quite fast and hit very well. He regularly led the team in doubles, but once he got to second base he'd

"Yup, Sunday summer sandlot baseball was fun. . . . when the 'moon' came over the ball field."

be all tuckered out and Gordon would have to devise some way—any way—to delay the game to allow the wheezing Bucky to catch his breath. About this point a fan would holler "Steal third base!" and Bucky would thumb his nose at him.

Bucky made the game fun. Some of his antics will never be forgotten, like the time when he went racing out to try to catch a Texas-league-pop-up in left field; he ran, then slipped, stumbled and fell and slid along the ground on his ample stomach—while his pants and drawers slid down to his ankles, revealing a shining posterior. The hastiness of his recovery was unbelievable.

From then on the fans greeted him with a variety of theme-songs: "Racing With the Moon," "Fly Me to the Moon," or, "When the Moon Comes Over the Ball Field."

Yup, Sunday summer sandlot baseball was fun.

When The 'Gloom' Collapsed On The Ball Field

Cars began leaving the ballpark, even though the game was technically still going on. But as far as the disappearing fans were concerned, it was over and their team had lost, 3-2. A wasted Sunday afternoon; time to go.

Not only was the game done with but also the season; and not only the season but also the championship, too; and not just a league title would slip away but the Grand Championship, a state amateur baseball title!

A pity, too, really. The Scandinavia Vikings town-team had experienced some excellent seasons; their won-loss record was superb, with division titles almost common. And even in the post-season playoffs of the past years the Vikings had advanced regularly up the bracket until getting bumped short of the title game.

And so a real pity this year. Never had the locals gotten this far before; never had they made it all the way to the top with a Grand Championship title and trophy and banner to bring to their tiny town. Perhaps a once-in-a-lifetime opportunity, and the Vikings had muffed it. No wonder some disappointed fans left the game early.

Back on the playing field the squad members themselves could reach out and palpably feel the let-down, the loss, the depression. They had made it to the top, but now they had dropped the big one—or as good as lost it. Just one more out and the whole thing was over. The cars kept leaving.

As the final batter began to stomp around and take his place in the batter's box, it appeared that only one person in the ball-park had the confidence that the Vikings could win, and that was the afore-mentioned team manager, Gordon Trinrud. Still the determined, eternal optimist until the last moment, Trinrud never let up in either the number or volume of words of encouragement aimed at the final hitter standing there fidgeting at the plate.

Even the raucous calls of desperate and disgusted fans to "PUT IN A PINCH HITTER!" were calls dismissed by Gordon, as he had no intention ever of bringing hurt or embarassment to anyone, and he had no intention now of downgrading the young man at the plate and making him come back to the bench, even if it meant Grand Championships. People came first; winning ball games was secondary. Trinrud was very special that way.

Meanwhile, the huge, hulking pitcher from the opposing team —Bonduel—began to smoke the final pitches past the nervous batter, but few paid rapt attention to the procedure. Virtually everybody was either leaving or making preparations to leave. Not only was the game lost, it was cold outside and it would be good to get inside.

Apparently even the Vikings batboy thought the end had already come as he began rounding up the loose Louisville Slug-gers lying around and started pushing them all into the canvas bat bag.

The despondent team members themselves, lolling about in the dugout, seemed about as optimistic as their alleged sup-porters streaming away in their cars. But why not go? After all, it was a 3-2 game, the last of the ninth inning, two men out and nobody on base; and their number eight hitter in the batting order, Keith Caldwell, stood there at the plate, the final batter of the game—and the season.

A few players began removing their spikes and putting on their street shoes. Several players were looking for their jackets and searching for their car keys, expecting momentarily to join the growing line of cars meandering slowly towards Main Street and then to the downtown taverns where they'd likely stop and take part in the final wake.

Yet that last batter kept fouling off one pitch after another and he seemed to be at bat forever. Good eye on that kid Caldwell. But only a few wayfarers hesitated briefly when the umpire hollelred "Ball Four!" and the intense Caldwell trotted to first base. Not much need to stop the exiting as the walk was just a fluke. Besides, the next batter was number nine in the order, so might as well be on the way before the big crunch of cars all tried to leave at the same time. After all, a big crowd, the biggest ever.

Then came a quick "Ball Four" again, and the batter, Lowell Peterson, lumbered down towards first, sending Caldwell to second. That event was enough to halt the walkers and make them turn back, while a few drivers who had turned on their motors now reached over and switched the keys to off position.

With this second walk the Vikings players came alive. Shoes and keys and even depression were set aside quickly. Something was happening, and maybe, just maybe something more and better might happen because coming to bat was their lead-off man, the tow-headed, pint-sized David Nelson, the team's leading hitter.

Squad members began hustling out of the dug-out to stand as close to Nelson as the umpire would allow as they shouted encouragement; fans also started getting out of their cars so they could see better; those standing behind the homeplate began moving directly up to and grabbing the thick-mesh screens in front of them. After all, that David Nelson—Little Nellie—just could do it; that sawed-off Norwegian could whop the ball a mile and he could run like a deer! Something actually might happen, and the tension mounted to match the anticipation.

"After all, that David Nelson—Little Nellie—just could do it; that sawed-off Norwegian could whop the ball a mile and he could run like a deer!"

The scene that three minutes ago had been one of gloom and doom became a moment of intense, nail-biting excitement. Not only was a tie-score possible, it seemed imminent! And after the tie, well, who knows? The answer to these maybes hung on Little Nellie.

And Nelson came through. He pounded a clothes-line double down the left field foul line, and the red-faced Caldwell never hesitated as he pounded around third base and headed home for the tying score, to be met at the plate by the entire team who pounded and belted the poor guy down to the ground in an orgy of happiness.

The stage was now set for ultimate victory. On third base stood the handsome Peterson; the diminutive Nelson stood puffing on second and grinning from ear to ear from his achievement and the wild cheering that affirmed as much. Just one more score and the Grand Championship would be theirs! Frank Merriwell could not have come up with a finish like this might be. Maybe.

To the plate now ambled the Vikings' skinny catcher, he with the loud voice; he with the round, thick glasses, the kid recently out of college who was starting his first high school history-teaching job. The guy sure didn't look like much of an athlete. He used a strange-looking bat, too, a Jackie Robinson style bat with the handle looking as thick as the barrel.

Whatever the appearance, the young catcher rapped the very first pitch thrown to him and he drilled a one-hopper right at the third baseman, but the ball hit the top of the glove and bounced away towards the shortstop who was too far away to field it in time for a play at first. Safe all around!

And Peterson came home! Peterson scored! Peterson brought in the winning run and the whole ball park went nuts!

The pretty fiancé of the catcher crawled half-way up the screen behind home plate; the wife of the pitcher began alternately to scream and to cry, a pattern repeated by many others. Over in the manager's box at third Gordon whooped and hollered and whooped some more and danced about and hugged players, and people grabbed and hugged each other and everybody jumped and hollered and cried and hollered some more. Pandemonium. Five whole minutes of gorgeous pandemonium!

Peterson's crossing home plate set off such a wave of hoopla and horn-honking and hysteria as to carry way downtown where those early leavers heard the shrieking sounds and wondered what in tarnation all that noise was about? After all, the game was over, wasn't it?

The game was over, all right, but not as the early abandoners expected it to end. And they missed it; they missed the big ending; they missed the biggest game ever won by the Scandinavia Vikings. It was quite a game, quite a day, a glorious day never forgotten by the players and fans involved.

LENGTHY POSTSCRIPT

The particular ballgame just described in part was more than a baseball contest, it became a historical event. It is still to this day referred to by those many persons directly involved as simply "the game," and that vague designation is all that is needed for the locals to know exactly what game is being referred to. This is true, even if it might have occurred some thirty years ago, as indeed it did, in 1954.

(There is a particular and partisan interest, of course, for this author about "the game," as I was the "skinny catcher" who brought home that winning run. Understandably, that day shall always remain one of my fondest memories. Also not incidentally, the next year I married that pretty girl who "crawled half-way up the screen," a remarkable act of agility she has not duplicated since that day.)

The point made about it still being called "the game" can be confirmed by noting that at the 1983 spring banquet of the

Scandinavia Vikings, the current team members, who are a generation removed from the event, had requested a discussion to include all the details of "the game," which was indeed done by including pictures and albums and newspaper clippings. (The 1983 newspaper report of this banquet referred to this portion of ancient history as "the glory days," and "the game" was discussed with a combination of love and nostalgia.)

As a current update on the other people mentioned by name: Peterson is a medical doctor and a noted heart specialist in Appleton; Caldwell is a successful mechanical engineer in Milwaukee, and "Little Nellie"—no longer so little—manages a farmers' co-op in Amherst, Wisconsin; Trinrud is retired and still lives in Scandinavia (see later column on Trinrud in Fall section). Also, not incidentally, a very large picture of that winning squad still hangs prominently where it has been hanging for thirty years, on the wall high above the bar in the tavern once owned by Trinrud, And, oh yes, Bucky Carr is yet single, yet a bartender, yet personable.

Every person should be so lucky as to play on one winning team in a lifetime. What kind of team or sport or non-sport does not really matter; it's just psychologically useful to have been with a winner just once. This success, no matter how trivial it might appear to others, does wonders for people for years to come; it does wonders for a community, too. And though everyone involved both then and now know perfectly well that it was "just a game," they also know that it was so much more than that for all of them. That victory serves both as fond remembrance and a subconscious reward that are always uplifting; it also serves as a cement to solidify permanently a group of people who shared a special moment. Memory is a fascinating and a wonderful thing; it helps us relive wonderful times, wonderful events, wonderful people. Minute as it surely is in The Great Scheme of Things, those aging players and supporters can conjure up a memory and say very quietly all their lives: "I was there, I was one of them, and I am very proud of it." American baseball has done strange things to and for its citizens. I know; I was there; I was one of them.

The Once Long Hard Road to Mecca

Like some 50,000 other people, we decided to go to Mecca, that is to Decorah, Iowa, for the three-day Nordicfest held there annually the last weekend in July.

The trip from The Lutefisk Ghetto, where we were visiting at the time, to The Norwegian Holy Land, was some two hundred miles and took a leisurely four hours in an air-conditioned car, with cruise-control, stereo-radio, and other amenities. There was a brief stop off the Interstate for an excellent lunch in an air-conditioned restaurant. Much of the driving involved cruising down four-lane highways on steel belted radial tires, and the entire journey was completed with simplicity, ease and comfort.

The trip to Decorah was not always like that; in fact, it was never like that; never simple nor easy nor comfortable; indeed, the drive was long, hard and miserable; it was a journey dreaded by our entire family, and we made that trip each year.

Because my grandfather's farm lay outside of Decorah, our family would go there from Wisconsin every spring as soon as school was out. Given the conditions of the times—the cars, the tires, the roads of pre-World War II—our annual trip to Iowa was more than a stressful journey. It was perceived at the time as a near incredible expedition because this pilgrimage of two hundred miles took all of the daylight hours and a portion of the darkness, too.

My father back then drove a black 1937 Plymouth two-door sedan, the latter inconvenience chosen deliberately to prevent his squirrelly kids from falling out of the back seat. There were four of us kids, my sister and two older brothers (I was "the baby," an opprobrious term that took years to outgrow); also the family dog came along to make her contribution to discomfort.

My mother prepared for the Decorah trip for days ahead of the embarkation. Because our family would be staying on Grandpa's farm for at least two months, extra everythings were brought along and these extras were packed both in seedy look-ing, taped-together straw suitcases, and large cardboard boxes which together were helter-skelter tied to both running boards. More supplies were stuffed into two bulging duffel bags which were drooped over each front fender and tied to the protruding headlights. A large canvas bag of extra water for the radiator hung from the radiator cap, while two wooden boxes of more clothes and supplies, as well as an extra spare tire, were strap-ped to the back bumper. The car-scene for the trip was a sight right out of **The Grapes of Wrath.**

Long before the sun was up on the day for the journey, we sleeping children were awakened, forced to eat a bowl of Ralston, and readied for the safari. Father had two basic lines to utter loudly just prior to leaving: 1) "Has everybody gone to the toilet?!" and, following tinkle-time, 2) "All right, everybody in, and let's roll!" His days in the Army in World War I still served him well.

10 Miles Down the Road

At this point in mileage came a question from the back seat that would be repeated many times, too many times, repeated to the point where father eventually reacted as though a sharp fingernail had been scraped down a blackboard: "Are we almost there yet?"

"NO! GO BACK TO SLEEP!"

25 miles

"Stop shoving!"

"Well, get over in your own place."

"Momma! He won't let me spread out."

Father: "STOP THAT FIGHTING! AND SETTLE DOWN BACK THERE!"

50 Miles

Sister: "Oh! How beautiful! The sun's coming up! Wake up, everybody; quick, look and see!"

Oldest teenage brother: "Huh? Ya woke me up just to look at some dumb sunrise? Geez, if you've seen one, you've seen 'em all. Goodnight."

Other brother: "I gotta go to the bathroom."

"Father: "I TOLD you to go before we left.""

"I did. Now I gotta go again. Bad!"

"Well hold it."

"I can't much longer. I been sitting with my legs crossed for half an hour. Remember what Gramps says? 'Can't hold what you haven't got in your hands.' "

Mother: "Please, we must stop, or we may have an accident."

Begrudging father: "Oh all right, then. This gravel highway looks almost deserted anyway at this hour. I'll stop by that grove of trees, and then all boys to the left side of the road and ladies to the right side. After that NO MORE STOPPING! Go in a empty coffee can if you have to."

75 Miles

"What's that loud noise? Sounded like a firecracker!"

Father: "Oh-oh, we got a flat tire. Must have picked up a nail. Got to stop fast or we'll ruin the rim. I'll pull over on the shoulder. Now you kids get out and play, but keep away from the jack!"

"Why?"

"Because I said so!"

100 Miles

"Open the windows. I'm hot."

"No. Leave 'em closed. I'm cold."

"I'm hungry. I think I'm dying."

"Me too. I know I'm gonna die soon unless I get sumpin' in my stomach. When we gonna eat? We've been on the road since Christmas!"

Mother: "We'll eat our lunch as soon as your father gets us to that clean roadside park just across the river into Minnesota."

"Are we almost there yet?"

"Just another half hour or so."

"We are?! Almost to Decorah! Yippee!"

"NOOOOOO! Almost to the Mississippi River."

When our chugging chariot came to and then crossed the big bridge over the river at LaCrosse, there was regular "oohs" and "ahs" and "look way down there!" But there was also the kid in the front seat (we took turns sitting in front between the folks) who gloatingly proclaimed: "Ha ha! I'm the **first** one into the new state—and you're last. Ha ha!"

"Well, we're the **last** to leave the old state. So there! Put that into your pipe and smoke it. Ha ha!" As the ensuing argument picked up momentum, Dad pulled the car into a roadside picnic area and fighting kids peeled out from the auto and into the open air as though they had been paroled from a packed prison cell.

The lunch was always the same: egg-salad sandwiches on home-baked whole-wheat bread, the egg-salad squished and running out at the middle (someone invariably sat on the shoe box containing the luncheon goodies); there was a ring of bologna, a half-moon of Colby cheese to carve, and a box of soda crackers; nectar (Kool-aid) for the kids and coffee for the parents; and chocolate cake for all. It was a great lunch.

Father always stood up while he ate and regularly he would walk over to the sagging car and then walk around and around it, kicking a tire now and then—which was a dangerous act of aggression, considering the baldness of the tread. Immediately after the last cake crumb got gulped down came the familiar words: 1) "Has everybody gone to the toilet?!" 2) "All right, everybody in, and let's roll!" Groans and moans accompanied the reloading, but again we were on our unmerry way lurching down the alleged highway.

125 Miles

"Why don't you play 'roadside cribbage'?" suggested the mother, slyly, sensing the growing tension and the near eruption of family members on the verge of strangling each other. Roadside cribbage was a diversion and a ploy that always worked to occupy kids' attention. It was a competitive game whereby points were assigned for farm animals seen along the highway. Horses, for example, were worth one hundred points, cows worth ten, while chickens were valued only at one point each.

Viewing a riding academy through finger-printed car windows was perceived as a veritable gold mine as all the horses brought a quick victory for that side that the critters were seen on. The only way to lose points in the game was to pass by a cemetery, a truly morbid experience as it meant one hundred points subtracted from one side's score.

Roadside cribbage went over well for about an hour or more but at some point the game would degenerate into another shouting match and then be halted forthwith:

"Hey! Look on my side of the road! Must be a hundred cattle in that herd."

"There are **not** that many; maybe twenty-five, thirty-five at the most."

"Are too a hunnert!"

"Are not!"

"Momma! He's trying to cheat me. I won't play no more. I quit!"

"Ohhh!! What's that noise, Dad? It's another flat tire! And we don't have a spare tire with air in it. Aargh! We'll be stranded here forever! Archeologists will find our whitened bones on the side of the road!"

Mother: "Shhhhh. Father, did you bring along the tire-patching kit and the hand air-pump?"

"Yah. Got it all in the bottom of the trunk. By the time we get everything out and fixed and back in again, it'll take over an hour. **Aa, drit i bukser**."

"Father! Shame on you! Talking so nasty!" exclaimed mother.

"WHAT'D HE SAY?" asked all the kids together.

"Never you mind. If I ever hear **you** kids talking like that, I'll wash out your mouth with soap." And she would, too.

150 Miles

"Hey, read that new set of Burma Shave signs to us, Dad."

"Listen, Birds, These Signs Cost Money, Rest A While, But Don't Get Funny. Burma Shave.' Not exactly poetic mastery."

"Momma, I don't feel good. My stomach hurts. I think I'm going to urp."

"Momma, if he gets sick in the car, he'll make me sick, too. Stop the car!"

Oldest brother: "Keep 'er going, Dad. Seems to me we stop this crate more than we start it. If Dummy over there is gonna barf, let him do it into that dumb straw hat he's wearing."

"Ya did too. You're ROTTON!" "I did not! I bet *you* did it.". . ."SETTLE DOWN BACK THERE! Or I'll whop you with a razor strap!"

The car did stop, however, and the unpleasant duty carried out in the roadside ditch, the mother holding the sick son, one gentle hand on the forehead, the other with a clean, wet rag wiping away the extra mess from the whitened face. The rest of the brood stayed in the car, grumbling—and all secretly hoping they wouldn't be the next victim of what was common car sickness. (There was one trip when Dad either couldn't or wouldn't stop in time, resulting in three of us almost simultaneously filling up our new straw hats, hats quickly abandoned on the side of the road. What a mess that was!)

175 Miles

"Oh-oh, what's that noise? Another flat?"

"No, thank goodness, just some bigger stones hitting the fenders."

"Oh-oh, look at that sign coming up. **Another** detour! Our third one today! Jeepers, I've seen cow-trails that looked wider than that detour road we're heading into. Bet the radiator will boil over again."

"Momma, the dog piddled. Stop the car!"

"Where'd he go on! Ah, it's not too bad, just went on the floor. Here, take this rag back there and soak it up a little."

"Me? Never! Pewey!"

Big brother: "That's not the dog who smells it up back here, it's you, Jerk, you let one. Ugh! Pollution! Open the windows!"

"I did not let one."

"Ya did too. You're rotten!"

"I did not. I bet **you** did it. A skunk smells its own hole first."

"MAMMA! Help me!"

"Ah, look, children, we're coming to the Iowa border."

"Yay! I'll be the **first** one into the new state. Ha ha."

"Well, I'll be the **last** one from the old state and Minnesota is better than Iowa. So there."

"It is not, and I think you're a big ugly drip."

"It is too, and I think you're a bigger, uglier moron."

"Momma, make him stop saying those awful things to me. You like him better than you do me."

"Well he started it."

"I did not. You did."

"SETTLE DOWN BACK THERE! Or I'll whop **you** ALL with a razor strap!"

200 Miles

"I'm hungry. I think I'm dying of starvation."

"Well I'm thirsty, and I **know** I'm dying for sure."

Mother: "Just hold your shirts on, both of you. Pretty soon now we'll be in Decorah and out on Grandfather's farm. You'll both live till then—somehow."

"Jeepers-Creepers, the sun's gone down. It's dark outside already! 'Course we've been driving since Halloween."

"I hope this jitney can make it up the Tesloe Hill just one more time," said the clenched-teeth father, more to himself than the carful of tired, antzy, thirsty, hungry, bored, fighting, fidgeting kids—and one worn-out mother who had spent the entire trip refereeing arguments, soothing jangled nerves, and supporting a frazzled driver-husband on the verge of collapse.

The car, in low gear, did inch up and over the Tesloe Hill, and in a few minutes we were finally but finally at the farm-gate. The dim car-lights swung off the county dirt road and down the winding half-mile driveway leading to the farmstead. In the distance we could see the pale yellow lights in the windows, a dull amber glow made from the kerosene lamps burning in the white, wooden-frame, square farmhouse. A few jolting car bumps farther on and we could make out the dim forms of Grandpa Lars and Grandma Julia standing by the swinging farm-gate of the farm yard.

The journey was over at last; the trials of the road had been met and surmounted; Mecca was arrived at. And then came the line from the teenaged brother: "Dad, let's turn around and go home."

★　★　★　★　★

Did you hear the one about the Norwegian schoolteacher?
She had trouble keeping her pupils straight! Yuk yuk yucukle.

FALL

"Klub," Controversial Delicacy

Scandinavians in America have a number of foods associated directly with their ethnic group. Certain of these foods are enjoyed by almost all people, including non-Scandinavians. Among these good-tasting items are pastries like fattigman or krumkakke or rosettes, and even a food like lefse is acceptable to most people.

Yet there are certain foods associated with Scandinavians that are not always enjoyed, nor even tolerated—and by some, not even worthy of the definition of food. Lutefisk fits into this category of being controversial; some folks love it, others hate it.

But there is one more controversial Scandinavian food specialty, a dish so unusual—and to some, so offensive—that even hard-line Norwegian spouses fight over it (Housewife: "I won't cook THAT for all the money in the world!")

By THAT is meant Klub. Not the Klub that is made out of potatoes as that's no issue or problem; it's the form of Klub made from—get ready—pig's blood.

In our Lutefisk Ghetto, blood Klub regularly appeared on family tables in the early fall, the time period for slaughtering animals to provide meat for the long winter ahead.

To us children, Klub was simply there on the platter, there to eat or not to eat. Klub being readily available was no big deal for kids who grew up and got used to its presence. To outsiders, however, the discovery of Klub's basic ingredient—the blood mixed with flour and butter and then "fried" and then cut into small strips to resemble a meat stew—could be a **devastating** discovery, as witnessed in the event of a teenage city girl named Annie Dybdahl who had come to visit her Aunt and Uncle on their farm for the weekend.

Now Annie, fourteen and fat, loved to eat. At the age between toys and boys, her first love was eating. Upon arriving, Annie breezed through Aunt Hilda's cookie-jar contents with reckless abandon, only to ask after eating the last crumb: "What's for supper, Aunt Hilda?"

"Vell, da men-folk yust butchered a hog, so. . ."

"So that means we'll have pork tonight, right?" interrupted Annie, who beamed at the thought of the evening's major course on the table.

"Vell, it'll be somethin' from a pig, dass for shoo-er," replied Aunt Hilda, not yet ready to tip off her menu.

At exactly five o'clock, they sat down on high-backed wooden chairs around a large round-oak table. In the center of the table burned one candle, right beside a mason-jar filled with a bouquet of black-eyed susans. Beside the flowers was a water-glass filled with teaspoons.

Uncle Gunnar began with the table prayer in Norwegian ("I Jesu navn. . . ."). Immediately afterwards, Hilda went to the kitchen and soon returned carrying a massive platter with all the meal on this one large plate. She appropriately set the steaming dish next to company, Annie, with the appropriate phrase: "Vaer saa god" (come and eat).

And Annie dived in, filling her plate with lots of everything, and she inappropriately began eating immediately. (Good Norwegians do not start eating until everyone has their food on their plates.)

"Hey! Mmmmmmmmmm! But is this ever good pork roast, even though it looks like stew-meat. Really grrrreat food, Aunt Hilda," said Annie between big mouthfuls.

"Vell, den, it's not really a roast."

"What is it then? Whatcha call it? asked Annie, still shoveling it away.

"Klub."

In an age between toys and boys, Annie just ate. . . and ate. . . until she found out what Klub was made of.

"Klub? That's a funny word. Never heard of that before. What portion of the pig is used?"

"Da blood."

"Blood? BLOOD! You're eatin'—I'm eatin'—BLOOD?"

"Yah-da, den. Tiss a special treat for company. Shoo-er glad dat yew like it" said Uncle Gunnar.

Annie's fat face turned white as she grabbed her throat. She jumped up from the table and ran out the back door with only the agonizing sound of "Arrrrrgh!" trailing behind her.

"Vell, den," said Uncle Gunnar, "Ay gass she din't like da Klub efter-all. Gewd! Dat means all da more for me."

"Yah-da, den," replied Hilda. "It came az a kinda shock, den. So tewmorrow, den, after yew butcher dose sheep, ve better not tell her 'bout 'rocky mountain oysters.' "

The Depression And Grade School Kids

"Did you brush your teeth, Lars?"

"Yah."

"Did you use baking soda or salt or soap?" asked the mother.

"Palmolive," answered the small boy. "Tasted awful—but my tooties are clean now."

"Did you put new cardboard in your shoes?"

"Yah."

"Don't say 'yah,' say 'yes.' Are you sure it's tough cardboard? Those are big holes in your shoes."

"Yah. I mean yes. I mean I cut the cardboard from a hat-box in the attic. I made double pieces, too, and they fit good in each shoe."

The mother then added a line said more with resignation than either anger or sadness: "I sure wish we could afford to get your shoes resoled. It's all the fault of the Depression."

"What's a Depression?"

"Uff da, it's too hard to explain. Besides you're too little to understand, so run along to school. But hurry right home after-

"Did you put new cardboard in your shoes?" asked the mother. . . . "Sure glad this Depression doesn't affect little kids". . . but it left an invisible scar.

wards and get your chores done. Remember!" she called after him, "you've got to fill the woodbox and carry out the ashes from the cookstove!"—but the young boy was out the door and gone before the final orders were heard.

It was a mile-walk to the grade school near the center of the village. At first Lars' shoes felt tight and funny-like because the new cardboard hadn't flattened out yet. But *ikke* worry (but not to worry), he thought; by the time he got there the shoes would feel just fine. And besides he knew that by the end of the second recess that there would be holes worn through the bottoms of both. Then he'd have to sit down, and take off the shoes and carefully slide the remaining cardboard either up or down to cover the holes once again. *Saa gar det* (so it goes), said Lars to himself, repeating a line his Dad always used. Yet he knew he dassn't get hold in his socks! Mom would have a conniption fit if he did!

"Then he'd have to sit down, and take off the shoes and carefully slide the remaining cardboard either up or down to cover the holes once again."

At the church corners he met classmate Trond Breistul, as planned, every day. Trond at the moment was swinging his Karo-syrup lunch pail around and around and his body was swirling about like a twirling dervish.

"*Hei, du* (hey, you), Trond. I got a question: What's a Depression?"

"I dunno—and I don' care. Hey!" he said, stopping his twirling, "Look at my new *bukser* (pants) my Mama made, and next she's gonna sew me a shirt from my aunt Katerina's old table cloth."

"Well, then, you ain't the only one to get sumpin' new," replied Lars, not to be outdone. "Look, see my coat my Mom made me from a window drape. And my cap she made from a trouser leg of my Dad's wool pants. It's real warm and fits just right."

By this time their friend Bendic Erickson had joined them for the final lap to the school house. "***Hei, du,*** Bendic, whatcha got to eat for dinner?"

"Same as you guys, I spose. A sandwich and an apple. 'Cept today I got rabbit meat, and better yet, bacon fat 'stead of lard on the bread. Lucky, eh?"

"Wanna trade lunches at noon?" asked a hopeful Trond.

"Maybe. Is either side of your bread the heel?"

"Yup," admitted Trond. "'Fraid so. Mama has to give the soft slices to Gramma, 'cause Gramma can't chew. No teeth. Gotta gum everything. She broke her old store-bought pair but sez she can't get new choppers on account of the Depression."

"Bendic," said a hopeful Lars, "do you know what a Depression is?"

"Maybe. Kinda. I know my mother cries a lot—though she tries to hide it. And our kerosene stove's broke and Pa says he can't fix it till he can get back on WPA. Right now he's out of work again. Pa says nobody needs a stone mason in the Depression."

Lars thought seriously about Bendic's comments, then agreed to share a possible problem with his pals: "My Dad tells us that if things keep on like this that our family is gonna end up on the County Poor Farm. What's that mean?"

"I dunno."

"Me either," added Trond, but he pondered an extra moment and then figured that he might add something to the issue presented. "Well, I do know my Pa ain't got money for no rent so we's first moved to another house, and then the sheriff came and then we's moved in with my uncle and his family. Geez, there's sure a lot of us. Three families in one small house."

"How's it going?"

"Okay, most of the time. 'Cept, uff da, when we go to bed, there's so many kids that we gotta sleep six to a matress, crossways."

"I sure wish I was rich," Trond then added with a sigh, "and be as lucky as the goofy Amund Gurholt. He's got a real metal wagon. With balloon tires yet! His family must be rich."

"Of course he's rich," replied the all-knowing Bendic. "His Dad's the rural route mailman."

"Are you sure mailmen are rich?" asked the doubtful Lars.

"You betcha they are. Mr. Gurholt gets a new car every other year, don't he? Know anybody else in town with a new car?"

"Nope. Nobody. 'Cept maybe Mr. Skurvik. He's got a sporty lookin' two-tone Buick, and that must make him kinda rich," observed Trond.

"Well, my Mom keeps telling us all the time that our family really is rich, too; that we've got everything except money. Y'know what that means?" asked Lars.

"I dunno."

"Me either."

"Confusing notion, all right," agreed Lars. "Just like the Depression. Sure glad this Depression doesn't affect little kids."

P.S. An update: Bendic is currently a cement-finisher in Evanston; Trond is a high school band teacher in Wisconsin; Lars is a university professor in Minnesota. As to the "rich" Amund Gurholt, he's a Dean at the University of Wisconsin. And all four still carry the invisible scar of the Depression.

Lost on the 'Scenic Tour'

A '27 Model-A Ford roared along the graveled country road, the car heading for the farm of one Gulbran Tvedt located somewhere in the Hitterdahl district.

In the car were Ivar and Ingeborg Lien and their two small children, Kari and Arne, and all had enjoyed the ride and the pleasant scenery along the bumpy washboard township road. But the ride was getting long. And there was one bigger problem: Ivar did not have the directions to the Tvedt farm totally clear in his mind. Mr. Tvedt had called Ivar a month before, inviting him to come some time and see his new place, and Ivar got the directions all right but the phone connection wasn't too good and amid the crackling of the wires and the noise of his hollering kids, he didn't quite catch all of the details on where to turn and when. This lack of information, however, he was not about to reveal to anyone. He'd find the Tvedt place, all right.

"We've been driving a long time, Papa. Are we there yet?" asked little Arne.

"Purdy soon," replied the father, "yust a li'l vays to go yet."

"Well, I sure hope so," said the mother. "Seems to me we should easily have been there by now. You sure know where it is, Ivar?"

"Yah-da, den. Yust keep yur shirt on."

Half-way up a long hill the Model A began to falter and die, and Pa shifted down into low gear, just as he'd done a half hour before when they had climbed the same hill.

"Hey," remarked Kari, looking up from her big-little-book that she was reading, "didn't we go up this steep hill already?"

"*Nei*. It's yust dat dey all lewk alike avround here," replied the father, giving quick support to the use of little white lies.

"Well," said the mother, chiming in on the subject, "I too could swear that we've gone up this same road before. Why don't you stop at the next place and ask directions, Ivar."

"Dere's no need for dat. Ay kin find it yust fine."

The car edged over the top of the hill and then started downward, the A-model suddenly picking up momentum and speed which pa wasn't going to restrain. Time and place were both against him and he had to make haste to find that elusive Tvedt farm. So let 'er rip, he thought, and he hung on tight to the steering wheel as the car tore down the long hill.

"Woweeee! Are we ever flying!" hollered Arne. "Bet this is the fastest this old buggy has ever gone!"

"Will you please slow down!" yelled the mother. "Do you think you're Barney Oldfield or sumping?"

"That-a-way, Pa! Open 'er wide open! Wheeeeeeee! Man-o-man but is this crate moving!" yowled Kari in delight.

Pa! You're lost!
Naw, yust a li'l bit turned around.
If you don't stop and ask directions, I'm going to scream!

"IVAR! I said to **slow down! And I mean it!** Are you trying to get us all killed? And look where we are now. I recognize this area. We're almost to Swede Valley! Are you sure you know the way?"

"Vell 'course Ay do. Tvedt sez to turn left at Benson Corners an' den right by da Gurholt scheese-factory and den left again by da four-corners past da Gausdal store. Or did he say right at Gausdal? Ay not so shoo-er 'bout dat las' turn."

"Then stop and ask somebody for directions," said the mother, firmly.

"Then stop and ask somebody for directions," said the mother, firmly.

"**Nei**. Ay kan find da place myself, den," said the father, more firmly.

"By the time we get there," said Kari with sadness, "we'll have to turn around and come right home again."

"Yah," agreed Arne. "And Pa, it's gettin' on to chore-time in about an hour."

"Ivar, please stop and ask somebody. Please."

"Ay tell yew dat ay kin git dere."

"Hey, Pa, I just saw a sign that said 'Scandinavia, 18 miles.'" said Kari.

'SCANDINAVIA!" yowled the mother in astonishment. "We're 50 miles from home!"

"Heh-heh," laughed Pa, weakly, "ay t'ought ay'd giff yew da scenic tour."

"Scenic-tour, my eye! You're lost. You've got us all lost! Admit it. And you're too stubborn to ask directions," said Ma, fit to the tied at this point. "STOP AND ASK DIRECTIONS!"

"Dare's no need."

"No need? What is wrong with you men? You're all alike! And worse than that, you're a stubborn Norwegian! They're the stubbornest of all!"

"Are we really lost?" wailed Kari to her father.

"Naw. Not lost. Yust a li'l turned avround."

The mother could take it no longer. "If you don't stop this car immediately and get help, I'm going to start screaming!"

"Me too," screamed Kari.

"Jeez, Pa. Do something to get us there," said Arne, sadly.

The whole family against him was too much for Ivar Lien to fight. He pulled into the very next farmyard, stopped, got out, went to the door, talked briefly, then sidled back to the machine and headed the Ford back the same way they had come.

"Now that wasn't so hard to do, was it," said the mother speaking somewhat carefully, knowing she was treading on her husband's bruised ego.

No reply. The car bumped along, no one talking for five minutes until Kari could stand it no longer:

"Know where to find it now, Pa?"

"Nope."

"Huh? What's the matter? What's wrong?"

"Dey're not home. Da 'hole Tvedt fam-ly iss avay wissiting her folks for t'ree days, and a neighbor iss doin' dere chores."

"Pa?"

"Yeah?"

"Let's go home."

"Yah-da, den. But it wuss a nice tour innyhow." No one replied.

Communication-gap Among Three Generations

WHAT'S IN A NAME? A Rose is a Rose is. . .likely called something else today.

To Amerika from the old country had come the Grandfather. When he arrived at his newly adopted nation, Grandfather had the special, mellifluous name of Tomartinius Skogsbakken.

That name was a bit too much for his first-born, second-generation son who eventually altered his own given "junior" title to read only Martin Skogen.

A Generation-Gap in Language. . . words don't quite mean
the same things anymore. . . . Turn down the stereo/the
record player/the phonograph. . . . "Ve vere all gay in dose
days."

Martin's son, who in turn might have been "Tomar-
tinius III," had changed his own family name even further
to make it sound even more American. The grandson
became just plain Marty Woods.

This one day the grandson, father, and grandfather sat
together and made pleasant conversation before being
called to eat lunch (Grandpa called it "dinner"). Marty,
recently graduated from college and back to visit "the old
folks," reflected not only a name-change for his genera-
tion but also a complete language-shift as well, as their
conversation suggests:

"As I was saying, in college we had a group who called themselves 'born-again Christians'," said Marty.

"In my day," replied the father, "we referred to these kind as
'charismatics.' "

"Yah-da," agreed Grandpa, "Ve had 'em tew, 'cept ve yust
called 'em 'holy rollers.' "

"Maybe," said Marty," these 'different" and 'forward' people
are now and were then simply 'trendy.' "

"They certainly seem 'avant garde,' " said Martin, the father.

"Vell, den," added Grandpa Tomartinius, "Ay tink dose kinds
of goofs are alvays sca-rew-balls."

"But first we should perceive what the Bible says before making any judgements," warned Marty.

"Indeed," Martin added, "we should first study the Scrip-
tures."

"O hoot-ma-toot," lamented Tomartinius, "nobody reads da
Gewd-Book inny more innyvay," and he waved off that sugges-
tion in disgust.

"Say, I see that Mom bought a new davenport for the house,"
observed the grandson.

"Yes, and I'm glad you noticed; it's a lovely couch. Don't you
think so, too, Granpa?"

"Me? Ay tink dat da ol' sofa vuss plenty gewd 'nuff for diss
outfit."

"Let's go out on the deck," suggested the grandson.

"Yes, that is a good idea to move to the veranda," said the father.

"All-vright, den, le's go sit on da porch."

"Before leaving, I think I better reduce the volume on the stereo," said Marty.

"Good idea. It was too loud, so please turn down the record player."

"Uff-da. Dat's da loudest phonograph ay effer heard."

"Hey, Dad, did you see my new digital? Neat, huh?"

"Say! That watch is a real beauty, a real hum-dinger."

"Uff-da. Dat's da loudest phonograph Ay effer heard."

"Humph! My time-piece serfs me yust fine. Lewk-a dis Eljin. Ay tell yew dat hven ay got dis 'un, it vuss wery nobby."

"Do you carry a briefcase to work, Dad?"

"Only a couple times a week is it necessary for me to bring my attaché case on my job. Did you ever use one, Granpa?"

"Oh ish-da. In my yob, dere vuss no need for no satchel."

"Oh, look! I see that Mom or you must have planted different shrubbery."

"Yes, the old bushes couldn't survive last winter."

"Vell, ay tol' yew dose scrub-cedars vere not tuff 'nuff."

"Ah, you can replace the shrubs easily, Dad. You're wealthy now."

"I certainly am not half as affluent as you might think me to be."

"Oh? Dat may be ta-rew, but compared to hvat ay had, ay tink yew're loaded."

"Is that a blemish I see on your face, Dad?"

"Yes, I'm somewhat ashamed to admit that I still have some acne problems."

"So das it. Ay figgered dose vere some fat pimples yew had growin'."

"With modern cosmetics, Dad, those blemishes can be covered nicely, and for added smartness, why don't you add a dash of scent to your chin, after shaving. Real macho, y'know?"

"Maybe. I suppose a touch of fragrance would be desirable and more sophisticated. Yet I'm not trying to give the image of being cool."

"Holy-smokers! Yew shooo-er vouldn't catch me puttin' on no perfume fer nobody. Only dose boyss who tink dey're girlss uses dat stuff."

"Ah, Gramps, I bet when you were young you didn't feel that way. Right, Dad?"

"Well, I know that in my own youth we certainly tried many strange things. Now admit to it yourself, Grandfather."

"Oh ya? Hven ve vere kidses, dere vuss no silly stuff. No need. Ve vere all gay in dose days. All uss boyss ver da gayest bunch of guyss effer."

"Granpa," said Marty, "I wouldn't touch your last line for anything. Let's go in and eat. . .er, dinner. Yes, Gramps, I'll bet The Gay Nineties weren't just named that phrase for nothing. Let's go."

City Versus Country: Avoiding the Facts-of-Life

There are a few pleasant advantages to growing older. Very few, maybe, but advantages do exist. Among them is the ability to view the childhood experiences in a far different manner than they were perceived at the time.

What today seems farfetched, naive, or simply old fashioned, made absolutely perfect sense at the time.

For example, when housewives (our mothers) soaked the dirty clothes over the weekend, washed them on Monday (and dried them on wooden racks standing over the heat-register), sprinkled them on Tuesday, and ironed them on Wednesday with flat irons heated on the tops of kitchen stoves, the whole process seemed as proper and natural as night following day. Time, in part, has altered all except the memories.

Now, years later, certain events in the early grades can be remembered with almost total recall. And in our lutefisk ghetto, where all the little fourth graders even cried in Norwegian, the tales they told then seemed perfectly logical:

When Sver Dybdahl reported that his uncle had killed an owl in a tree by walking around and around the tree while the owl kept twisting its head to watch him on every circle, we accepted the conclusion that the owl had indeed twisted its own head off and so died.

When the teacher asked Rasmus Tollefsrud what was the most beautiful thing in the whole world, and he responded with "a platter full of torsk," we could nod in agreement that his position had merit.

When Anna Aanstad reported that her grandfather had gotten on the wrong train that was going to Chicago instead of Minneapolis, we were ready to believe grandpa's reply to the conductor when informed of his problem: "Vell, don't tell me, tell da engineer."

We believed, of course, as fourth graders in this town of almost 500 people, that we were rather sophisticated because we attended a "city school" that had four rooms, while our brethren in the outskirts went only to a one-room school (which was always painted white, not red).

Yes, we were city-slickers. After all, our school had a six-holer outdoor biffy! With real toilet paper (well, most of the time). And we had a stone-crock drinking fountain that held ten gallons of water. And we had store-bought bases for the softball field.

"Yes, we were city-slickers. After all, our school had a six-holer outdoor biffy!"

Alas, those short-on-civilization country kids only had two-holers (and Sears Roebuck); and they drank out of a dipper from a pail, and their bases were gunny sacks half filled with sawdust. (And sometimes they had girl pitchers on their softball teams. And, worse yet, those girls often beat us!)

"When Sver Dybdahl reported that his uncle had killed an owl in a tree by walking around and around the tree. . . we accepted the conclusion that the owl had indeed twisted its own head off and so died."

What ever the fairness of school comparisons, we thought then that true worldliness infected our classroom. Why, we even had two members who not only had traveled out of the county, but had even gone out of state. They had been in North Dakota! For most of us, "taking a trip" meant going in late August to that big town 25 miles away to get school clothes.

We still believed, however, that pure cosmopolitanism permeated our small class. After all, did we not all engage in cryptanalyses with our secretdecoder rings obtained from the radio program, "Captain Midnight?" Did not our belts hold inaccurate hikeometers—which came via Wheaties box tops and ten cents—from "Jack Armstrong?" Did not every boy's overalls hold a special jackknife with the imprimatur of "Tom Mix?"

Truly, we were "with it" in American culture. Why, a couple of kids even maintained, with an air of know-it-all, that they were reasonably sure where babies came from, other than those brought by the stork, of course.

Then came our comeuppance. It took a country school transfer named Truls Anderson to straighten us out in a lesson on anatomy—and himself in a lesson on how to shock social sensibilities.

We were instructed by our teacher (she was an old lady, almost 25!) to draw a picture of a horse, "one that looks like a real horse," she directed clearly, much to her later discomfort.

When we were finished with our crayon work, we were each to walk up to the front of the class and display the artistic results.

Now fourth-grader Truls Anderson had lived on a real farm with real horses. He knew his subject matter well. And so when he paraded forward and held high his 14 by 16 inch picture, done in stunning yellows and browns, his real horse included real genitalia, of considerable proportion, it might be added. (Indeed, in retrospect, Truls' perception of reality lent credence to the concept of the Myth of the Giant Penis.)

The poor teacher was mortified. The class went into semi-shock. The girls averted their eyes; the boys looked for a hole to jump into. All except Truls, of course, who was a little slow to catch on to all the fuss.

When it finally dawned on Truls as to what had happened, he got a bit testy, and he rebutted the negativism around him with a perfectly rational rhetorical defense of his masterpiece, and he delivered his supportive evidence with the proper brogue he had learned at home:

"Das da vay dey lewk, yew dummies."

Afterwards, the event made us ponder the good possibility that country kids knew more about the real world than city kids, after all. And for the rest of the year we wondered suspiciously why the teacher insisted that we draw only pictures of rabbits and squirrels.

Yet we knew why. So it was goodbye to realism, hello to euphemism in both picture and word. Sophistication comes in strange ways in fourth grade.

The Joy of Telephone—Listening

In some rural areas about the time of the Second World War, the hand-cranked telephones on the wall had a device attached to the phone which allowed anyone to listen in on conversations without being heard by those talking on the phone.

At a time when many farms had no radio, no daily newspaper and, of course, no television, the telephone became a major means by which news of all kinds could be learned.

With often a dozen or more parties on the same line, this permitted all the phone owners on that line to eavesdrop on all conversations. Everybody listened in on everybody else. That practice was readily understood by all, if not always appreciated. (Although some tried it, it did no good to break into Norwegian from English as one language was as easily understood as the other.)

For some patrons of the phone system, there was an understandable reluctance to divulge either private thoughts or privileged information, and for these people the conversations

were usually brief, purposefully vague, and occasionally involved communication bordering on secret codes.

These latter type of non-conversations were dismissed by my
listening grandmother (1866-1956) as a combination of dull-
ness and insult. Or as she once phrased it after banging down
the phone in disgust:

"Vel, den, nuttin' effer happens when Mrs. Tongen talks to
Mrs. Kirkeby. Dose tew talk goofy-talk. A couple of stuck-ups,
if yew ask me."

The kind of conversation-listening that Grandmother enjoyed
the most occurred rarely, that is having a call made by some
stranger who was not aware that the whole neighborhood was
listening in. So when these special moments came, it was pure
joy for Grandma. A regular bonanza! A new-found fortune, a
unique moment when the unvarnished truth would be spoken;
almost a Fourth-of-July-like celebration of a Private Confession-
al gone public via the phone lines. She loved every morsel and
tidbit and responded to all the news by talking to herself about
what she was hearing.

In retrospect, Gram's newsworthy phone calls, along with her
side comments, are today solid cultural history; but at the time
they were simply pure heavenly bliss for her.

This was one of those calls as Gram, her ear implanted in the
receiver, related the lines of some unsuspecting stranger who
was telling all:

"Hoo hoo! Dey're sayin' dat Knute Lovik iss gonna git married
to da oldest Aasen girl. An' he ain't even asked her fodder for
permission yet! *Aa den store verden!* (Literally "'Oh the big
world!" but used primarily as a very common idiomatic expression denoting surprise or dismay.)

"Now he's tellin' dat Rasmus Moen's coussin iss takin' da train
all day vay to Minn-ap-plis yust to wissit an art museum. *Aa
den store verden!* Can yew tink of anyting so dumb to do?

"An now he sees dat Thorvold Gunderson iss tew payments
behind to da bank on his new tractor. Serves Thorvold hvright.
He don' need dose new fangled contraptions. Horses iss da best
for da land.

"Herre Gud! (Holy God) Marin Tollefson iss haffin' a baby at Ca-riss-mus! Seems to me she yust got hitched in Juni. Lemme scheck da calendar 'bout dat one!"

"*Herre Gud!* Marin Tollefson iss haffin' a baby at Ca-riss-mus! Seems to me, she yust got hitched in Juni. Lemme scheck da calandar 'bout dat one.

"Oh may gewdness! Did ay hear hvright? Yup. Tiss ta-rew. Sigvart Lien iss sendin' his boy to town to high school next year. My my my my. He'll be da only one from our township at da Academy. *Aa den store verden!* But den da boy ain't no good on da farm, so dey might yust as vel send him someplace, and school can't hurt him tew bad.

"Vel, den, vould you believe dis? 'Snoose' Bakken iss gettin' his vife a vash-machine vit an 'lectric motor. Uff da. Ay bet dere light-bill vil double! Da vay some folks spend! Vunder hvat dey gonna use for mooney? Corn stalks?

"But den da boy ain't no good on da farm, so dey might yust as vel send him someplace, and school can't hurt him tew bad."

"Now dey talk about dat vild dance in town las' Saturday night. *Aa den store verden! AA DEN STORE VERDEN!* Oskar Skurvik poked Poos Hanson in da snoot! Bet it vus da boose dat pumped him oop. *Nei* (no). Da fight vas over dat jung Skretvedt girl. Fee-da. All dose Skretvedt girlses iss nuttin' but trouble-makerss. An loose morals dey got. Dey say every las' vun of dem smokes like a shimney.

"*Aa, nei nei nei.* Iff dat issn't da berries, den. Hjalmar Hovdal has got to take his brudder Odvar to da store effrey veek 'cause Odvar don't know how to drive a car. Hvat kind of a man iss dat? A sponger, dat's him. Iss Odvar some kind of cripple or sumpin'? 'Course Hjalmar iss rich. He drives a four-holer Buick.

"Ah, shoot. Dey're gonna close-off now. 'Tiss chore-time and da cows iss vay back in da pasture and da vife iss goin' after dem.

"Vell, Ay gas Ay better call my sister Eunice (pronounced Jew-niss) 'bout tyin' quilts in da morn. 'Cept ay hate to call on diss phone. Da nosy neighborss iss alvays listenin' to tings ve talk about."

The Most Intelligent Illiterate

The sales clerk eyed him suspiciously. The shabby-looking man had been standing by the store's card-rack for fifteen minutes looking at card after card, and those cards without pictures he often held upside down.

The clerk did not know what to make of him. Who would stand and try to read over and over again a greeting-card held upside down? The guy certainly appeared strange. And seedy. And maybe retarded.

To the distraught clerk, the disheveled man in the aisle looked like some dumb country hick who came to town twice a year for groceries, and then went back to the barnyard. This day the man had brought some of the barnyard to town; she could too easily tell that from the manure on his eight-buckle overshoes and the barn-smell on his tattered clothes. She surely did not want to wait on this ignorant galoot.

He was a big, red-faced, rawboned man, and the clerk could see his large arm-muscles pressing against his thread-bare mackinaw coat. He seemed so out of place; he looked as though he belonged only behind some plow or down by the pigpen slopping the hogs. Why must this strange-looking, foul-smelling stranger stand there fingering one Hallmark card after another?

"Why must this strange-looking, foul-smelling stranger stand there fingering one Hallmark card after another?"

Calloused hands that looked like dirty roadmaps kept picking up and laying down every card in the display rack. Those cards with pictures of babies he looked at the longest; those without pictures he kept turning every which way.

At last the clerk decided that, regrettably, he would not just go away, as she hoped. She finally felt compelled to go and wait on this dunce from the brush, just to get rid of him.

"May I help you?" she asked, forcing a pleasantry towards him, but staying back herself far enough not to be contaminated.

"Yeah. My vife yust had anudder baby, an' ay vant to git her a purdy card an' say sumpin' kinda nice." Then he turned away and mumbled, "'Cept ay don' know hvat to say."

Oh Brother, thought the clerk to herself. The rich get richer and the poor get kids. And here's a half-wit foreigner who can't even talk right. Yecccch, she said sarcastically to herself, on the eighth day God created Norwegians.

"That's nice," the clerk, however, felt herself replying. "May I suggest that you write her a note on the bottom of some appropriate card?"

"Vell, to tell da troot, ay neffer learn how to hvrite—'cept ay kin spell my name."

Just as I suspected, thought the clerk, now trying hard to figure out the quickest way to get rid of him. "Well then," she smiled weakly, "just find a card with an appropriate verse, sign your name, and send that.

"Vell, Ay can't vread, eeder. Vould yew pleassse vread dem cards to me?"

Ohhhhhh, the clerk groaned to herself. An illiterate! Read him cards? I should have known better than to even wait on him! But now she was stuck, so bravely she asked, "What communicative message do you wish to convey?"

"Huh?"

"What do you want to say to your wife?" Her exasperation was starting to show.

Tiss our fourt' baby girl. Das all ve git is girlses. 'Cept ay don' care. Girl-babies iss fine vit me. Ay luff all babies. Das hvat ay vant to tell her."

"Huh?" This time it was the clerk who was taken back.

"Tew minny men vant only boyses. Such hussbands iss dumb. A man an' vife shewd be happy ust to haff inny kidses at all. 'Spesh-ly iff dey're healt-y babies. Effrey birt' iss a mir-cle. Hvat yew tink?"

"Yes, yes, yes," answered the clerk hastily. "I think you are so right. And I think it's wonderful that you feel that way. I only wish more husbands felt as you do." My goodness, she thought, this weird figure makes marvelous sense.

"Vell, den, ay luff my vife. She iss fine voman. A kind, decent luffing, Christian lady who luffs us all more dan innyting. She sess so effrey day, and da 'hole fam-ly giffs hugs to each udder effrey morn."

The poor clerk now didn't know what to say. She had so obviously misjudged this smelly figure, this extraordinary man.

" Y'know?" he added. "Inny baby iss God's vay of sayin dat da vorld shewd go on." He then stopped to ask again: "Vould you pleasse help me find a card for da missus?"

And so she began to read the cards to him. Many cards. Many messages. And together they would smile, and together they would laugh, and together they would discuss the card's message and then seek yet another card that might better give the right meaning. And by now the clerk was not bothered by any sights, and smells, and together they found just the right card.

At the cash register the farmer paid for his purchase, then tucked the special package into the breast pocket of his bib-overalls. Turning to go, he added: "Y'know, ay gotta tank yew. Yew nice lady, tew, like my vife. Minny folks iss not kind." He then paused, took a pinch of snoose from a Copenhagen can, then said: "Da human vorld iss a funny, messy, sort of place in hvich mos' pee-ple yust bumble along mos' of da time. Dey don' see inny but dere own li'l bit a' logic, an' dey stick to it no matter hvat da reality avround dem may be."

The clerk felt somewhat in shock. She wished she had a tape-recorder to get his message; he'd analyzed the human condition far better and more simply than any philosophy book she had read.

"Vell, den, das life azz ay see it. Seems to me dat ve shewd all try an imitate Christ. Den da vorld vould be a better place," he concluded, and out the front door walked the most intelligent illiterate the clerk had ever seen.

'Takk' for Trinrud's Tavern

In the 1940s some people still called them saloons; others said taverns; a then-modern term for the same thing was "bar" as the phrase cocktail-lounge had not yet caught on.

Whatever the exact title, these business establishments sold liquor, wine and beer, primarily to male customers. (It sometimes took either a brave—or a fallen—woman to enter through doors where booze was dispensed by the glass over a bar.)

The image of the tavern-keeper in many towns then was such as to rank him just behind used car salesmen for trustworthiness and just ahead of paroled convicts for moral accountability. Indeed, some church people doubted the feasibility of even accepting the tavern-keeper's money in the Sunday collection plate. "Tainted," they called it; "immoral income," some said; "corrupt money from a den of inquity," others concluded.

In our Lutefisk Ghetto, however, any harsh judgements toward the tavern-keeper were unfair, unkind and untrue. The man who ran the primary tavern (there were only two bars in town) was both an honest and honorable man, and in many ways he was superior in his daily Christian living to those alleged Christians who condemned him.

Only now, in retrospect, can one see that this small-town tavern was really a multi-purpose establishment which met the basic needs of the entire community. The place served many social functions ranging from a senior-citizens-center (in mornings), a community-gathering place (in the evenings), and a communications-center (both day and night).

The tone of any business place is set by the owner. The host figure in the tavern was named Gordon Trinrud, a second-generation Norwegian-American. In an atmosphere regarded often as crude and vulgar, Trinrud's bar was different. He allowed no cursing, no rowdiness; there was never a fight because he nipped any possible altercation in the bud with a stern Scandinavian voice: ***"Pas det, du!"*** (Watch it!)

Without coming close to a psychology or economics book,

Trinrud succeeded mightily because he possessed three basic ingredients, each in large proportion: 1) common sense; 2) integrity; 3) a kind heart.

★   ★   ★   ★   ★

A routine day in Trinrud's small-town tavern:

By 8:15 the retired farmers in town—and a few still-active farmers who got their milk-cans already delivered to the creamery— are at the "senior citizens" card tables where game after game of whist gets played, with Trinrud alternately refereeing, kibitzing, and sometimes sitting in briefly for someone who drops out for a trip to the lavatory or, as it's often phrased, "Gotta see Missus Jones, den."

With the age of the card players, Norwegian is often spoken and Trinrud can **snakke Norsk** with the best of them: **Nei, men, har du set slik?''** (No, but have you ever seen such a hand?)

Knowing both drinking capacities as well as the wallet-sizes of all his clientele, the owner dispenses appropriate amounts of fermented beverages to each participant—and carefully cuts each off at the right time, but never doing so in a way to make anyone lose face.

(For all his fair and sound judgements, Gordon has won even the grudging admiration of the housewives left at home, most of them eager to get their men-folks out from under their feet for a spell. "Takk," (thanks) they say privately and quietly for Gordon, but never to him.)

By noon the card-players have left, and the place becomes the News-Headquarters for men dropping in for a quick nip and the latest information: "Iss da auction on da Melby farm T'urssday, Gordon?" "Nope, it's Friday; starts at 1:30." "Takk." "Vuss dat Nottleson **gutt** (boy) hurt in dat accident by Smoocher's Hollow, den?" "Naw, him and the Gudmandsen kid tried to staighten out a curve, but nobody got a scratch on 'em." "Takk." "Hass Karl Jorgens stopped tradin' eggs in hiss store, den?" "He'll take eggs but don't want no more chickens." "Takk."

By one o'clock the tavern turns into the Community-Phone-Information Center: "Hello, den, Gordon? Iss dat yew?" "Yah." "Iss Tomartinius Mork in da ga-rage tewday?" "Not this after-noon 'cause he heard the **karuser** (blue gills) were bitin' in Sand Lake and he took the afternoon off. "Takk." "Hello Treen-rewd? Are yew dere?" "Yeah, I'm here." "Vell, hvat time iss da pie-social startin' at da schurch?" "Goes from one to four-thirty." "Takk." "Hei du (hey you), Gahr-dawn? Iss da ballgame diss Sunday at home or avay?" "It's out-a-town." "Takk."

Among phone calls, a fast sandwich, a quick-look at the sports pages and scattered customers, the place is readied for the afterwork rush. A fresh 16-gallon keg rumbles in from the back room and gets maneuvered amid grunts and snorts and puffs into the cooler and tapper apparatus; clinking glasses get dumped six at a whack into smelly chlorinated vats; spittoons and stools and cleaned ash-trays are shoved into their proper positions. The "family room" is ready.

By 4:09 the railroad section crew is lined up along the mahogany, the four men hunched over just alike; they look alike, dress alike, talk alike, and Gordon knows each alike. How much railroad work got done today? is the standard question, and the response is standard' "Aaaaa! Ve all vork like ca-razy men!" And everybody laughs alike, and Gordon sets up a free round, and all alike say "Takk."

A high school boy, hot and thirsty, sidles in nervously and asks haltingly for a bottle of pop. Legally the kid cannot be in there because he is neither 21 nor with his parents. But the one restaurant is closed down (for good, as is turned out) so the considerate Gordon brings the boy the Pepsi but with it comes his special look which the kid understands perfectly: I'm not supposed to serve you anything, so drink it down quickly; and don't you dare move ten feet from the front door! The lad guzzles down the pop gratefully and when he turns to leave, his own eyes fall on Gordon and the boy's eyes too say "Takk."

The button of a bib-overall pops loudly, the owner reaching in for both his snoose-box and a fat billfold, the latter from which he extracts two hundred dollars. "Hei, du, Gur-din, Ay vant yew hold diss till Ay git back frum da voods, den. Ay not vant to loose my **penger** (money)." And Gordon takes the cash and puts it where it will be safe. "Takk," the man says. They both know the money will be safe. The whole town knows the money will be safe because the tavern is more than a barroom, it is a community institution operated by an honorable man.

Most people in retirement are not thanked for their work in their jobs, and it seems certain that saloon-keepers are thanked even less, if at all. But there are many people who have special memories of how Gordon Trinrud improved their lives. Me included. He was what Presidents or Governors or Kings or Congresses can never make, a kind and caring person, a gentleman and a gentle man.

Thus to an ex-bar-owner of a tiny tavern in a tiny town, there is imperative need for a brief commendation which comes some thirty years late but is no less sincere: "Takk."

The Sin of Gluttony—
Lutefisk Suppers

This was it; this would be the day; the long-awaited event was almost here—the annual fall Church Lutefisk Supper.

Some of the chairmen of the food committees were already at work in the church kitchen by sunrise. It would be a long day—and night.

By the time Edna Gudmandsen hurried into the church at 7:30, the efforts of her potato-peeling crew had reached the point where Edna was dumping the peeled red Russets from pails into vats and then from vats into wash-tubs. The huge amount of potatoes might seem staggering to some, but Edna knew that by midnight the potatoes remaining would fit back into that single pail with which she started.

By 9 a.m. the church kitchen began filling up with ladies, all chattering amiably, all concerned about their specific tasks. In one corner Dora Trinrud had her cole-slaw committee at work;

in another corner was Amelia Voie's group in charge of peas and carrots. In the center island stood Elsie Nottleson counting the cartons of pies, and as she tried to get an accurate number, people kept coming in with more and more pies, all of the pies donated, of course.

Over two of the stoves in the main kitchen stood Selma Hanson, the lady in charge of the meatballs, and at the moment the ten heaping vatsful sitting clumped together didn't seem to be sufficient. And would there be enough gravy?

Mabel Peterson came struggling through the kitchen dragging a huge plastic garbage-bag filled with enough cut-carrots and celery sticks to feed the entire county, but her only concern was running out of them the way she did three years ago. Mable dragged the sack past a cardtable set up temporarily for Magda Mork who was preparing the cranberry sauce to be served in soup-bowls, and there didn't seem to be enough cranberries there to suit Mrs. Mork.

Standing on a high stool was Alma Johnson piling package after package of buttered lefse on top of a big brown ice-box to the point where the last box of lefse touched the ceiling. Alma liked working with lefse much better than with rutabagas, her assignment last year. Then again she and all the ladies knew that any food-job in the kitchen had to be better than having to prepare the lutefisk.

Ah yes, the lutefisk preparation. That particular function was for and by men only; it was hard physical work. Chairman Loren Wrolstad had literally been up the entire night opening fish crates, filling vats, filling tubs, cleaning fish, moving the slippery fish from one watery container to another; and also filling the kerosene stoves, too, with enough fuel to last until midnight, the approximate time when the last ticket-holder would get fed. Loren hoped that there would be enough fish left by midnight for himself to eat.

The lutefisk preparation was deliberately placed in the room farthest from the main kitchen. Despite the name of the supper, the ladies did not want their particular parts of the meal stunk up by any unnecessary lutefisk odors. And smell it did, smell through the entire church, and would still smell in the building two weeks after the supper had ended.

The lutefisk-room was normally the kindergarten classroom for Sunday School, but for this one day and night it was a lutefisk factory, a space set up like an assembly line, one wall lined with stoves, the other with multi-tubs of cold water, copper boilers with hot water, and in every container there was lutefisk, sometimes dry, usually wet; sometimes hot, sometimes cold. There seemed to be enough fish in that room to feed the entire Norwegian navy.

By noon the preparations of all the foods had proceeded far enough so that workers knew that together they would make it all work out, somehow; together they would keep the tradition going yet another year, somehow; together they would work and work some more for this one special meal; they would make it again, somehow.

The Lutefisk Supper did not begin officially until 3 p.m., but automobiles were filling up the church parking lot by 2:30. The cars came from everywhere, from out of state as well as out of county. Many former area residents chose this special day to make their annual visit home, and they knew the process and procedure well:

First, get to the church as soon as you got to town and buy your $2.00 ticket; hope for a low-numbered mimeographed ticket which would allow you to wait only an hour or so upstairs before being called to eat downstairs.

Even inside the foyer of the church the procedure would not change. At the ticket table would be Winfield Krostue, and Krostue would be jovial, laughing, full of jokes, and sucking on a dead cigar.

Then with your ticket you move into the church proper and sit in the pews. And sit, and sit some more. And wait, and wait some more; wait for the special man to walk up to the front, that man who was the high school principal, he of strong voice

"The Lutefisk Supper. . . . And smell it did, smell through the entire church, and would still smell in the building two weeks after the supper had ended."

and no-nonsense manner; this man of authority would read off ticket numbers in his loud voice, after which two, seven, maybe ten more people would be permitted to get up and start walking downstairs to a table just abandoned by some stuffed eaters who had eased and oozed themselves away from food that had no end.

Now for the slow walk downstairs to the eating place. Though you cannot see it, you know that rushing women are cleaning off your table and setting new place settings. When you turn the first corner you can hear the loud din of clattering dishes and the babble of voices; when you turn the second corner you can at last see the crowded room, the tables pushed close together to get more people in; you can watch the scurrying high school girl waitresses who are all so young and so pretty and dressed all alike in their Scandinavian red vests, white blouses, and black skirts.

And finally you are escorted to your table, your own wooden-folding chair to sit on, a Lutheran Brotherhood donated napkin to place on your lap. In front of you is a warm plate and the still-hot silverware just back from the dishwashers in the kitchen. And lying there beckoning are the newly filled bowls and saucers and platters of food. Everything is ready!

A moment of hesitation as the strangers at your table glance up at each other. But enough of formality. Without a word it's **vaer saa god**, come-and-eat, dig-in; it's pig-out time. Pile high the blistering-hot boiled potatoes and pat a fat hunk of butter into the middle of the mound; surround the pile with hot peas and carrots and rutabagas; fill in a spot with cole slaw; let the celery and lefse rolls hang out over the side of the plate because there must be enough room left in the middle for the lutefisk.

Yup, there's the steaming lutefisk there on that big platter. It's wiggling and jiggling by itself just lying there! Good sign. Slip and slide a large portion on your plate. Then take that pitcher and pour the melted butter over the fish; then keep on pouring until the whole plate is one golden pond, with islands of food sticking out in this sea of melted butter—waiting to be eaten.

Oops, mustn't forget to salt. Salt it all down; salt it some more for good measure. Now you're ready. so eat. Don't talk; people don't come to lutefisk suppers to talk. Eat it all; gobble it down. Then fill your plate again, and maybe again; same ritual, same quantities. Catch the fleeting waitress for some more scalding coffee. Keep eating; save only, but only, enough room for the pie.

At last you're full. Too full. It's ironic as you realize that the Sin of Gluttony is on royal display in a church basement. Oh well, it's only once a year. Time to push back the chair; time to grab the napkin for the final time and wipe away at the grease and gravy. Time to look up and see the crowd of hungry people standing in the stairway waiting there quietly but impatiently for their turn at your table. Time to get up and go, even if it's hard to walk. Great meal. Must do it again next year in 1951. Wonder how many years they can keep this up?

It's midnight. The church basement is empty except for one table of white-aproned, weary eaters—the kitchen staff—the men and women who had been there since morning.

Some of the food is entirely gone—out of cold-slaw at 8:30, meatballs disappear by 10—and the remaining portions are luke-warm as well as sparse. Mainly just bones and skin left of the lutefisk. Group reduced to filling up on rutabagas and lefse. Skimpy meal for those who had worked so hard, and they know it.

But together they also know that they have accomplished a hard task; together they realize they have made another supper another success; together they admit they are bone-tired; and together they are relieved that the supper is finally over.

Tomorrow and tomorrow they might look back and find the annual Lutefisk Suppers rewarding, worthwhile, maybe fun, maybe even wonderful. But today—rather tonight—at midnight the suppers mean only extra work, too much work, and they all silently know that the tradition will be ending soon, real soon. The young people aren't interested in keeping the suppers going; they say there's got to be an easier way for the church to make extra money. They're right. But still it will be a sad day when there are no more lutefisk suppers.

"O Lutefisk"

[May be sung to the tune of "O Tannenbaum"]
(written *circa* 1950)

O Lutefisk... O Lutefisk... how fragrant your aroma
O Lutefisk... O Lutefisk... You put me in a coma.
You smell so strong... you look like glue
You tast yust like an overshoe
But Lutefisk... come Saturday
I tink I'll eat you anyvay.

O Lutefisk... O Lutefisk... I put you by the door vay
I vanted you to ripen up... yust like dey do in Norvay
A dog came by and sprinkled you... I hit him vid an army shoe
O Lutefisk... now I suppose
I'll eat you as I hold my nose.

O Lutefisk... O Lutefisk... how vell I do remember
On Christmas eve how we'd receive... our big treat of December
It vasn't turkey or fried ham... it vasn't even pickled spam
My mudder knew dere vas no risk...
In serving buttered lutefisk.

O Lutefisk... O Lutefisk... now everyone discovers
Dat Lutefisk and lefse makes... Norvegians better lovers
Now all da world can have a ball... you're better dan dat Yeritol
O Lutefisk... vid brennevin (brandy)   (health-medicine)
You make me feel like Errol Flynn.

Fear and Trembling in the Melon Patch

"Hey, you two guys wanna go along coonin'?"

Such was our invitation to steal watermelons. In our area, the curious term for pilfering melons was "cooning," an expresion whose word-origin was lost in time, but very likely had ethnic overtones. (At the time we gave the word little thought; it was simply a nice phrase to use in place of stealing.)

The invitation for a melon-patch raid was made to me and my friend Oscar Moe. The invite came on a Friday night, I recall vividly, because the next morning was our confirmation-class at the only church in town—Lutheran, of course—and Oscar and I were two thirteen-year-olds who were expected to study our lesson on Friday nights for church the next morning, the lessons being a memorization of portions of **Luther's Small Cate-chism** and Luther's explanation of the Commandments, The Creed, et al.

(Oscar's real name, by the way, was Gene, but like several other boys, he was called by his father's name as it had a special ring to it.)

What was so special in our invitation to purloin melons was that it came from those we regarded as "the big boys," namely two senior high youths and one real oldster—age 19—just out of high school. For them to ask us "kids" to go with them on this nefarious mission was to us a badge of honor. We had arrived at manhood! Not only would we be going with aged, experienced cooning-crooks, but also we would be raiding a full-scale, multi-acred melon patch located between two towns. (Waupaca and Manawa) south of our lutefisk-ghetto.

Admittedly Oscar and I had engaged in minor cooning before this big-time offer came along; we had nabbed a striper or two from some local gardens, but our cooning came among the cucumbers and carrots and squash and was pretty petty thievery. Somewhat strangely, our garden-raids had an element of morality because our set—the junior high crowd—stole only what we could eat afterwards at one sitting, and no more.

Indeed, taking more than could be stuffed down afterwards was regarded as improper. Thus watermelon stealing was "right" if you only took a few and ate them, and it was "wrong" if you cleaned out the whole patch and stored them for a later eating party. Such were the situation-ethics and the complicated standards of us teenagers. (Was it Martin Luther that made us so "moral"?)

The major hitch to both Oscar's and my going with the "old pros" lay with a parental curfew; that is we both had to be home by ten o'clock. For most of our community, the world stopped for the day at ten p.m. and did not re-start till the next morning at six a.m. Anything done between those black hours was thought to be done by those of questionable moral character, an assumption that may have been correct.

Anyway to the original question: "You guys wanna go coonin'?" came the immediate query from Oscar and me: "Ya gonna be back by ten?" Now our future brother-robbers showed nothing but contempt and disdain for our question, because not one of them had to be home by ten o'clock or even midnight! These guys were FREE MEN. We were teen-aged slaves, held in escrow by our parents, and farmed out for mental-torture on Saturday mornings when five-hundred-year-old Martin Luther still wreaked his revenge on mankind by requiring pimply-face children to memorize his entire **Catechism**. Martin held a second mortgage on our lives.

"Yah, we'll be back by ten, easy," sneered the driver, who had to add, "so your Mommas can tuck you two under your blankets."

Dismissing the cutting sarcasm, Oscar and I looked at each other. We both wanted to go. After all, this was Big Time! Out with the Big Boys! Cooning from the Big Patch! And the certainty that we would be home by ten p.m. made the invitation irresistable. "Yah, you betcha, we'll go along," we said with strong affirmative tones that hid our already nervous feelings about what might happen.

Our co-nabbers included the Kirkeby boys, two brothers, and

Torben Erickson, always but always referred to by his nick-name "Muddy." It was both coincidental and different that all three young people could speak fluent Norwegian—this in the late 1940s—while Oscar's and my Norsk vocabulary was some-what limited to swear-words.

Anyway, we all piled into the Kirkeby Pontiac—which Muddy pronounced "Poonchack"—with us B-team twosome in the back seat while the A-squad sat in front, despite the inconve-nience and squeezing caused by the massive shifting mechanism in the middle of the floorboard. But they had to sit together or how else could they show their status? None would deem it worthy to ride with those sniveling kids in the back seat. Nothing but amateurs back there, me and Oscar.

While the car roared along, the front-seat plotted strategy and tactics while the back-seat neophytes leaned forward and lis-tened with respect to their elders. The scheme was to come up to the melon patch—which field ran along state highway 54—from a back sideroad, leave the car half a mile away, go by foot through a corn field to within fifty yards of the melons, and go the remaining distance on our bellies through a clover field.

Why all the hard work? Why not a daring raid: zoom right up to the field, screech to a halt, rush into the patch, grab some melons, and be back in the car in thirty seconds and blast off out of there? Why not? Because there were armed guards on each end of the melon-patch, that's why. And each guard car-ried a loaded gun! Really? Yup, the front-seat-mafia said so, and who were we to doubt them? The one guard reportedly had a shotgun, the shells loaded with rock salt; the other man had a .22 automatic rife, the bullets loaded with beeswax.

While neither firearm would kill you, you'd be a walking-wounded-kid afterwards, or so said the experienced voices from the front-seat to the two thirteen-year-olds who suddenly began wishing they had stayed home to ponder their **Catechism** lesson.

Too late now. Our Poon-chack meandered down highway 54 so we could first "case the joint," and we cruised slowly and in-nocently by the melon field, a field that was at least ten

STEALING WATERMELONS versus LUTHER'S SMALL CATECHISM

telephone poles long! The biggest patch we'd ever seen! The greatest potential payoff ever offered melon robbers! (Did John Dillinger ever get a similar feeling?) Oscar and I looked so hard that our eyeballs were ready to pop out, but we saw no guards and suggested as much. "Dey're dere!" said Muddy angrily. *"Er du galen?"* (Are you crazy?) Well, if Muddy says they're there, they're there, lurking in the dark shadows and fingering the safeties on their guns.

At that point from the front-seat come an announced decision that was worse than hearing about armed guards: "We'll wait till dark before we hit it." Wait till dark? Oscar and I looked frantically at each other because we knew the meaning of those awful words; it meant we wouldn't get home by ten o'clock! And armed guards would be nothing compared to unarmed parents.

But what could we say? If we said to go grab the melons now, we'd be *galen*—and maybe get a blast of rock-salt in our rear ends; if we said that this is all a big mistake—heh, heh—and that we want to go home, we'd be branded "chickens" and suffer humility from our peers for ages-on when (if?) we ever got home again. We said nothing.

The car was driven off the highway and on to a gravel road where we circled back and then parked the Poon-chack in a remote grove of trees. There we sat waiting for darkness to protect us hoodlums. To kill time we tried to smoke cigarettes, but because the back-seat didn't know how to inhale, the front-seat wouldn't give us any more cigarettes. The front-seat told raunchy stories; the back-seat laughed, but the laughter was hollow. Sometimes we didn't understand the sophistication and hidden nuances of the rotten jokes, but mainly our thoughts were less on Ole-and-Lena and more on home and Luther's little **Catechism** which somehow began to seem more interesting and important, especially if one were sitting in a safe home studying. Stomachs knotted, fear grew.

We wished fervently that we were home. How/why did we get ourselves into this mess? Crime-Does-Not-Pay, we learned by listening to Gangbusters on the radio, but now we were in CRIME up to our Norwegian blond hair. Pay? It would be hell-to-pay, that we knew for sure. We'd either get shot here or shot at home when we got back late for curfew. But at least at home we would die in the comfort of our own living rooms.

Finally but finally the sun set, but as the sky darkened in the west, it lightened in the east. A full, harvest-moon right off a creamery-calendar-picture shone over the melon patch. It was half light out; the guards would shoot us for sure! We'd be wounded and maimed. And then the cops would come and arrest us! Argh!

But there was no more time to ponder our future jail cell; the moment for sin had arrived, and we eased out of the car, closing the doors gently. From the trunk came dark-colored coveralls and black stocking caps which we all put on. Then in single file we headed for the corn field, walking slowly, listening intently. Muddy turned around and whispered an extra bit of information that we could have done without: "Hey, den, be quiet. Dey got police-dogs der det'll tear youse apart." Oscar and I pretended to take the news manfully, even though we were both ready to faint dead-away on the spot.

At the edge of the cornfield we peered ahead and tried to make out the dim melon-field ahead of us—and locate the guards and their dogs! While we were searching, suddenly a loud shot rang out and I fell to the ground in fright, and a body fell on top of me. It was Oscar. Which of us was more scared at the moment would have been hard to measure. We hoped the Big Boys didn't hear any whimpers.

"Hey youse gice," mumbled Muddy, "dat wuss a truck back-firin'. C'mon, let's get the loot." They got down on their stomachs—Oscar and I were already in that prone position—and we crawled on our bellies through prickers and sand burrs and moldy clover, finally arriving at the edge of the fabled patch itself.

Each body squiggled forward, the orders being to get far into the center of the patch to find the biggest and best melons, and to test their ripeness before taking them by thumping them hard with the knuckles. Oscar and I squiggled and wiggled all right, but grabbed the very first melons we could feel, and we squirmed as fast as we could back to the clover field, half carrying, half pushing two melons each. Test them for ripeness? Never! The German Shepherds would hear the thumping and attack!

The sweat was running and the breathing came hard by the time we reached the cornfield, where we could stand up. But we were still alive, so Huzza for big favors! We glanced at our Mickey Mouse wrist-watches; it was ten o'clock on the dot. Holy Hannah! And two Catechism-scholars still fifteen miles from their safe bedrooms. Back home we knew they were worrying about us; at the moment we were worrying about them.

Nevertheless we believed that we would soon be on our way. That's what we thought. But no! Orders-From-Headquarters came down to say to go back in the patch again for more! Take more? We didn't need any more; we had plenty to eat already. Take more? That would be immoral, maybe downright wrong. But showing the backbones of chocolate e'clairs, Oscar and I followed orders.

So back again, same route, same sand burrs, same fright, same results, same weariness. And then we made a third trip, and a fourth! This wasn't simple cooning anymore; it was grand larceny!

At last our elders pronounced "Enough," and then began the bone-wearying trips from the cornfield to the car and back again carrying the heavy green melons. Hard work, but Oscar and I moved with alacrity because the sooner the car was filled, the sooner we'd get home.

The stolen fruit in our possession filled all of the trunk and most of the back seat, too. Oscar and I sat on top of the piled melons to the point where we had to stay bent over, and still our backs hit the car roof, but at least we were heading for home, glorious home, and yet what awaited us there we knew well: unarmed parents with murder in their hearts.

Oscar got dropped off first and then made the miraculous discovery that his father was out of town that night (he sold silos), a joyful discovery indeed, because Big Oscar could and would have taken the razor strap to his wayfaring son. Oscar's mother was a warm, indulgent lady whose kindness matched her considerable girth, so after a few semi-harsh questions and statements about his whereabouts, he was ordered to sit down and study his **Catechism.**

While going for his book, Oscar heard a loud voice at the door. It was my father looking for me! He barged into the room to find a play-acting, nonchalant Oscar pretending to be study-ing Luther's righteous instructions, but my father knew that Oscar's concentration was somewhat limited because Oscar had the book in his hands turned upside down.

By this time I was home and lying in bed pretending to be sleeping. When I heard my father come noisily into the house—with doors banging and quickening footsteps heading for the stairway—I knew the scam would end quickly. It did. He came bounding up the stairs three at a time, burst into my bedroom, and, though he was a small man physically, picked me up out of that bed with one arm and shouted what would normally be a reasonable question: "WHERE WERE YOU!"

And I responded with what would normally be a reasonable lie used many times over: "At the movies. We couldn't get into the first show so had to wait till the second one, and it just let out."

I don't think he believed me. Perhaps my ashen appearance was the tip-off. Maybe the look I had of about being ready to throw up tempered his wrath. Anyway, he did show the graciousness to drop me, and back on my bed I landed. Then came his Declaration-of-No-Rights, a normally reasonable posi-tion to be taken by a distraught parent pleased beyond belief to see his child still alive, and angry beyond redemption at that same dumb kid for causing him such a scare. I knew what he'd say, and he didn't disappoint me: "YOU'RE GROUNDED FOR A MONTH!"

So ended the Great Melon Raid—for Oscar and me. What about our co-conspirators in this scheme? That same night the other three went over to the lake in town to a spot called "Smoochers' Hollow," and there they busted open melon after melon on the bumper of the Poon-chack and gorged themselves for over an hour on the red, sweet, sticky substance. A regular orgy.

Indeed, they had so many melons still left over that all the town kids had melon-eating-parties every night for the next week, but did Oscar and I ever get to one of them? Nope. He was grounded too. Neither of us got to taste one morsel of the forbidden fruit.

There may be a great lesson from this particular trauma, but I'm still trying to figure out what it is. Yet ever since that event, and to this day, I still prefer cantaloupe over watermelon. I don't like Poon-chacks either.

High Church, Low Church, Anybody Home?

The small, white, wooden-frame church stood on the highest hill in the rural township, and from this location the two figures could see for miles around them. The two of them stood at the top of the church steps, the one a young boy of twelve, the other the boy's elderly grandfather.

"Sure a pretty view," said the lad, surveying the farming region in the distance. "I bet we can see a hundred different places from up here. The whole scene looks like a patch-work quilt that Gram made."

"Yup, little 'rug pieces' everywhere you look. Nice view, all right," replied the old man as he too marveled at the panoramic picture of green fields, red barns, stave siloes, and white farm houses as far as the eye could see. "Many people say this area looks like the old country," he added.

"How's so?" asked the boy, both out of curiosity and respect. The boy had just arrived from the city to spend a week with his grandparents.

"Well, then, with Norway having so many hills and mountains and little farms tucked in here and there, this area here resembles it, that's all." The aging man prided himself in his

Yah, the church service was O.K. The music was good but the commercial was too long!

manner of talking; he had purged any ethnic dialect from his speech and took offense at the many people he knew who "still talk that way," as he phrased it.

"Jeepers! You can see at least five churches from here, Gramps. What kind are they?" asked the boy.
"Oh, then, they're all Lutheran, of course."

The boy hesitated in his reply, then asked: "With not that many people in this area, how come they needed so many churches?"

"That's kind of hard to explain. . ." said the old man, thinking at first to duck the question, "but to tell the truth. . .well, the early settlers fought a lot over religion, and this led to different families starting and going to different churches." There, he said it, and it was true.

"Well, did you always go to this particular church?" asked the boy, getting more curious and plotting at the same how to keep getting honest answers from his namesake.

"Nope. Didn't always attend here. When I was about your age, my father—he was an immigrant—he got mad 'cause the high-church folks in his church started to try to run everything. There was a big scrap and Pa quit and then we started coming to this place. Yup, those high-church Lutherans were too pushy for Pa. Practically Papists, they were."

Now the boy was really confused. "Do you mean the building was too high, or what?"

"Nah," laughed the grandfather. "It had nothing to do with sizes of buildings."

"Well, what exactly brought on the split? Must have been something awful important to make your Dad so angry."

Grandpa paused, stroked his chin, adjusted his wire-rimmed, round glasses, then shook his head. "To tell the truth, I can't remember the major issues." But he added: "They sure were mad at the time. I remember neighbors not speaking to each other. We'd meet local folks on Sunday morning in their horse and buggies on their way to church and we'd not so much as wave to each other."

The confused young boy pursued the interesting discussion but gave it another slant. He pointed to a decrepit-looking church just a half-mile down the hill where he could see the windows were boarded up. "When was that place last used?"

"Lemme see, now. That church quit about the time old man Kirkeby died. His family was the main bunch that kept it going. When church mergers took place, he kept his church from ever joining any other synod. Stubborn Norwegian. He was a tough old bird, though, and he liked his religion tough, too. Church services for him were a waste if they didn't last over three hours." Then the old man laughed as he thought of something.

"What's so funny?"

"Ah, I was just thinking how old man Kirkeby and my father used to go at it in our summer kitchen. First one would pound the Bible and holler; then the other one did the same, only louder. I recall Kirkeby left our place with his nose so bad out of joint that he and Pa never spoke to each other again. Ever!" He then added: "Never did like the Kirkeby clan myself, either. Stuck-up old geezer; a jumpin'-Jesus-nut, that's him." Grandpa was having obvious trouble with his temper.

The grandson had never heard such nasty talk from grandpa before and he wondered if he should keep questioning him. He decided to hang in there:

"Well, what did your Dad and this Mr. Kirkeby split over?"

"I'm not really so sure anymore. But I do remember Pa gettin' red in the face and telling old man Kirkeby he was 'headin'-for-hades.' Say what you will, and to be fair 'bout this, both men knew their Bibles backwards and forwards, even if neither one ever finished grammar school."

"How did all this affect you?"

"Pa, he gave me strict orders never to play with the Kirkeby kids. We didn't either. We really got to dislike each other even though we never talked forth and back. Also I was never to play with the neighbor boys on the first farm down past our place 'cause the folks there played whist. Worse than that, the daughter there got hitched and had a wedding dance. And that same gal wore rouge and lipstick and Pa called her a regular 'Jezebel.' "

This last line was too much for the younger generation representative who now asked defensively: "What's morally wrong with card-playing? or dancing? or wearing make-up?"

"I dunno any more. I used to, though. I know Pa wouldn't allow no painted-ladies around our house. He had a whole long lists of 'Thou shalt nots.' My Pa, he was a low-church man, a true Haugean."

"A what?"

"A follower of the beliefs of Hans Nielsen Hauge, a lay-preacher in Norway who got into hot water with the state church in Norway. Even went to jail for his views."

"But. . .but that's another country. Why was this Hauge so important in America?"

"Well, I can't just remember any more. I do know that just the mention of his name made some people around here jump for joy—and others just jump."

The startled boy began to shake his head in amazement. "I keep hearing about 'the good old days' but they don't sound so good to me. Seems like Christians didn't act very Christian around here."

"Yah, it was kinda sad sometimes. And if somebody here married a Catholic, it was regarded as the End of the World. Whole families also broke up over that predestination issue."

"But weren't you all Lutherans?"

"Yup. Sure were. Of one variety or another. That's why there's so many churches. Every faction had to have their own place of worship."

Still unbelieving and confused, the boy said once again: "But I still don't understand exactly what they were fighting over."

"I gotta admit that it beats me, too, nowadays as to what all the fuss was about. But it sure seemed to make sense at the time! And I still don't like the Kirkeby family to this day," added the grandfather loudly, pounding one fist into the other. "In fact, I hate 'em!"

"But why?" pleaded the boy, hoping for some reasonable explanation to this whole historical mess.

"Well, to tell the truth, I can't really remember."

Thou Shalt Know Thy Neighbors—And Their Faults

They had once been high school classmates, but that was twenty-five years ago. At the moment they were standing on main street, there on the sidewalk and curb just outside the local funeral parlor, trying to converse.

It was the funeral home visitation that by happenstance brought them together for this impromptu meeting, but their visiting was made almost impossible because of the interruptions caused by cars driving by them, the occupants of which invariably waved "helloes" to the one man, a local resident who was born and raised in the town and who had not left the area for any length of time for over forty years. He knew everybody in town—and everybody's business—and everybody knew him, hence all the waving at the cars' occupants.

The other person had also been born and raised in this community, but he had moved away after high school and hardly ever came back, this funeral being a rare exception. The absent former resident got an ample dose of local history, each lesson prompted by a moving automobile with waving arms and hands at the windows.

"Hey, then," said the local man, turning back to his former classmate after a flip of the hand towards a Chevrolet moseying by, "You remember those people, I'm sure. That was Alfred Hotvedt and his wife Hannah. They used to live on the Amundson farm but moved to the Wolden place 'bout ten years ago, Yah, you gotta remember Alfred; he was a sport. Played the fiddle at all the local old-time dances, and Hannah was a darn good dancer, too. Real light on her feet for a fat woman."

"Well, no, I can't really remember either one."

"Sure you do. Their cuckoo daughter Ingeborg—she used to be so wild—she married one of the Skogen boys. They live on the Kjendalen place now. Got a whole raft of kids, too. A regular brood-sow, she wuss. You musta knowed her old man, Lester Skogen. You recall the Skogen boys?"

"Were they the ball players who were so good?"

"Naw, you're gettin' them mixed up with the Skowen family. The Skowens were the good baseball players; the Skogens were, well, they wuss good at drinkin'. . ."

"Anyway, where were we before that interruption? Oh yes, our high school days."

"Hey, then, remember our senior year? That wuss sumpin' special! 'Member that crazy cheer we dared the cheerleaders to do? They did it, too! Woooweee, that was a goofy thing. I 'member it went like this: 'Lutefisk and Lefse, Rømegrøt and Sild, Who'll Beat These Guys? Our Team Will!' " (His attention then became diverted by another car and four waving hands.)

"Oops, there goes Johann and Severin Melbo in their new Buick. They made it big in potatoes last year, that's why the new car. Had a hunnert acres of Red Russetts alone. Borrowed money from his uncle Torben for seed and fertilizer. Torb's a great spender. He sess 'money is like manure; it ain't no good 'less you spread it around'. Anyway, the Melbos rented the Karlstad farm. Paid too much rent money, if you ask me. Anyway, you remember them, of course."

"Well, not really. It's been along time since I lived around here. Is their farm in the Swede Valley district?"

"Huh? No no no. Their place is just south of the Gullickson Hill. It's on county trunk G., just off highway 49, or you can get there from 161, too, if you cut just south on the gravel road past Omey Hoyard's farm. I'm sure you recall the place. Got three siloes on it and. . .Hey! There goes 'Screw-Loose Skretvedt' in that old Plymouth of his. Wotta wreck! Can't afford a decent car. Spends all his wages in the taverns. Regular bar-fly he is. Still says that same line before throwin' down a shot of boose: 'Time to clean out the flues'. Hey, then, you just have to remember 'Screw Loose.' "

"No, really, I can't recall anybody named 'Screw-Loose.' "

"Ah, heck, that wasn't his real name, of course. It was Edwin, but only his Ma called him that. Lemme tell you 'bout him and his wife and how they fight in the bars. . .Oh, oh, do you see that car? See it? Look!"

"Yup, I'm looking."

"Lemme tell you 'bout him and his wife and how they fight in the bars. . . Oh, oh, do you see that car? See it? Look!"

"That's the Dobbe brothers. You remember them. Anyway, they bought that car at Junction. Traded in three heifers and two pigs to buy that Chevy. Can you 'magine a car-dealer takin' in **griser** (pigs) on trade? Purdy strange, if you ask me. But them Dobbe boys are dumb like a fox. And tight. They'd trade in their old lady on a John Deere if they could get a good deal on her fat body. Everybody knows how tight they are. They squeak when they walk. **Penger** (money) pinchers. Maybe welchers, too. They say. . . . ."

"Say, not to change the subject, but what are you doing for a living?"

"Me? Ah, shucks, same thing I've always done. Farmin' most of the time and drivin' a little truck for Wolding on the side. . . Say, look see quick! That's Ida Anderson. You know her. Poor thing lost her husband 'bout five years ago. He was out in the field and just hookin' on the combine and he drops over. Just like that. Dead as a doornail. You knew him. Gunnar wuss his name. Course everybody called him 'Snoose.' Yup, Snoose Anderson. Great guy. But him and Ida never had no kids. Strange. Nobody could figure out why. 'Course you remember old-man Lysne, that smart-ass, he wuss gonna ask Snoose if his Ma ever told him about the birds and the bees, 'course he didn't. Most of us figure it was Ida's fault, but old-man Lysne figures that Snoose didn't know nuthin' 'bout how babies were made. 'Course nobody knows for sure; didn't dare ask. Get a

"Hey! There goes 'Screw-Loose Skretvedt'. . . . and you MUST remember Walter Skurvik. 'Skurvy Skurvik?' Now THAT was a character!"

punch in the snoot. Anyway, Snoose sure left Ida with a nice spread, though; nice place, I'd sure like it. You must know their farm. You head out the B-road, then take a left at the Bestul School, then north on Double A. . ."

"Sorry, I don't know where the Anderson place is either."

"Well Bald-headed Nellie! You must be gettin' forgetful in your old age!"

"It's been twenty-five years!"

"Well hell's-bells, nothin's changed. Same everythin'. 'Cept 'course a few folks croaked and a few kids got born, and a few deserters like you moved away to the cities. Sure didn't think you'd forget us though. . . . . Well-well-well, now wouldja look at that machine just comin' round the corner. You've GOT to know them folks, just GOT to."

"Well maybe I should. But I don't."

"Y'mean you don't recognize the Gurholt outfit? Both their girls were in school with us! The girls they got married right after high school. 'Course one of them had to; got in a family way. One married a Sannes, the other a Borgen west of town. Both hard workers. The Gurholts were related to a former neighbor of yours, the Evansons. Mrs. Evanson was a sister to Mrs. Gurholt, and their husbands were cousins, too, though only third cousins once removed. Now you just HAVE to remember them!"

"All I remember is that I can't remember."

"Well Jumpin'-Jehosephet, man, you sure forgot us! 'Course as a city-slicker, I s'pose you know hundreds, maybe thousands of people."

"As a matter of fact, I don't even know the names of the families who live on the same apartment floor that I'm on."

"Y'don't? Really?"

"No, I don't. And what's more, I don't care to know them either."

"Well wha-da-ya-know-'bout them berries! I just can't 'magine not wanting to know 'bout your neighbors."

"I'm sure you cannot. You've demonstrated as much." But the old acquaintance was not listening. He was intently watching a faded blue Ford careen around the corner. "Hey, then. I think that is. . .YES-SIR-REE-SIR, it's him! It's 'Dill Pickle' Swenson! We used to be on the same bowling team. Haven't seen the likes of him in a whole month! Still drives like a madman. But great guy, that Pickle. Drinks a little too much. Gets a little ornery, too. Still one keen Norskie, you betcha. Lemme tell you 'bout Pickle. . ."

"Well, er, ah, it's geting late."

"It is? By George, you're right. I gotta run; gotta go; gotta pick up the missus and go out for chicken-in-a-basket and chili. Gonna meet Carsten and Dora Jorgenson for supper, too. Hey, I bet you know Carsten. He's a shirt-tail relative of mine. His aunt Gladyce Hanson married my second cousin Walter Skurvik. You MUST remember Walter Skurvik. 'Skurvy Skurvik'? Now THAT was a character! Lemme tell you about HIM. Hey, where ya goin'?"

"After twenty-five years I do remember an old Norwegian line from around here: 'It sure wuss nice wisiting—but now tiss schore-time.' Bye. See you at the next big funeral."

"HOME ON DA FJORDS"
**(Ode to *Syttende Mai*—17th of May,
Norwegian "Constitution Day" 1814)**

Melody: Home on the Range

O give me a home. . .where the Norwegians roam
Where the torsk and da lutefisk play
Where seldom iss heard a non-Norwegian word
Because it is **Syttende Mai.**

(chorus)
Home. . .home on da fjords
On the day we chased out dose Swedes
We made dem guys run. . .like a son of a gun
We ran them right out t'rew da weeds.

Today iss da day. . .dat da Norskies all play
They will chew all da snoose dey can find
They'll drink lots of Glog. . .and yump like a frog
Becoss it sure helps them unwind.

(chorus)
Home. ..home on da fjords
Where Fattigmann iss a big treat
We make rømmegrøt t'ick, till we almost get sick
And dat lefse sure cannot be beat.

(chorus)
Home. . .home on da fjords
Where da oil-wells and gammeløst are
So happy I'll be. . .in my old Model T
It's da best doggone Henry-Fjord car.

Why don't you and I. . .on da Syttende Mai
Take da day off wit da rest of da bunch
When it's Brudderhood-week. . .instead of a Greek
Wy not take a Norsky to lunch?!

(chorus)
Home. . .home on da fjords
Where da torsk and the lutefisk lay
Where seldom iss heard. . .a non-Norwegian word
Becoss it's da Syttende Mai.

Rufus and Kjitel Knew All About How to Hunt Deer!

The process of Americanization has, over the years, eliminated much of the Old World heritage for the present generation, but for the first and second generations growing up in rural America in the 1930's and '40's, that heritage was strong and ever-present.

Both the heritage and its effects came out every autumn in our lutefisk ghetto during the deer hunting season when it was mandatory to (1) shoot a deer, and (2) outwit "dose city sa-likerss." Hence a brief scenario from the past:

The Red Coats are coming! Herre Gud! The season is here! Every able-bodied man is expected to be out deer hunting; the written law of manhood requires it. The only excused males in town are the lame, the halt, and the blind. Any others who remain at home peek out furtively from behind drawn curtains and avoid appearing on the streets until after dark.

As to Non-Hunters: "Dey're all a bunch of schickens!"

Another unwritten law of deer hunting holds that deer are to be found "up north," or as it's sometimes pronounced, "oop nort." Any deer found south of town are abberations, likely some misguided critters who strayed from their proper northern habitat.

Alas, but also straying oop nort to our town are "dose damm city fellersss" who, according to the locals, can't hit a bull in the rear with a frying pan, and get so drunk that they can't hit their own rears with both hands.

"Dat's ta-rew," says Rufus to his neighbor, Kjitel Moen, "dose gice iss dainch-rus! And dey shoo-oot our deer! Tiss a toff sit-ew-a-shun but vee got to face it. An' fool 'em." And so they plot strategy.

Anything negative about any deer season is to be blamed either on hunters from the cities or the state conservation department.

The latter is a favorite whipping-boy of the barroom biologists like Rufus and Kjitel.

"Dem yewniwersity pee-pol read tew many boo-ooks," says Rufus.

"Yah-da. Akaret (exactly)," agrees Kjitel. "Dose books yust sca-rew up dere heads. Uff da."

Conversations on how to shoot a deer, how to outwit their city cousins and how to flaunt the conservation department can be witnessed by tuning in on Rufus and Kjitel at the local tavern, "Little Norway," the night before the season opens:

"Vell, den, haff yew got yer buck all tied up for da morn?" asks Rufus.

"Yeah, yew betcha," replies Kjitel, who leans over to whisper: "Aye tink dere'll be deeres yust below da barn," and he pauses to look around for foreigners before adding: "cus aye poot a salt-block out dere las' veek, den," and he smiles the all-knowing grin of complete assurance.

"Hoot-ma-toot!" says Rufus in mock astonishment. "Aye gas dey'll be dere den," and he adds the expected and proper rationalization: "Ve feed dem all da time vit corn an' oatses an' cloafer an' tim-o-tee hay, sew dey're yust like owning our heffers."

"Yah-da, den. Yew kin say dat agin'," says Kjitel, in appreciation of this commonplace, if nefarious, scheme.

"Know sumpin?" says Rufus, and now it's his turn to look around for strangers. "Aye got my buck las' veek, a seffen-pointer dat's been feeding vit my Yersey cowss in da back forty. Yimminy, but vuss aye effer pussled ven aye first saw dat buck, den!" Rufus leans back and concludes: "Da missus hass it canned in yars in da fruit cell-ar already."

A big car pulls up outside and stops in front of the tavern. Out pile six hunters all dressed in their new red outfits. They stop in to check on the hunting and have a few drinks.

Soon two free bottles of beer sit in front of Rufus and Kjitel, who sit patiently awaiting the question that they know is coming. Finally: "Hey, you guys know this area pretty well. Are there many deer around this town?"

"Nope. Dere ain't no deer around here, den. Dose dummies in da conservation department haff rooooooned all da huntin'." says Rufus, with proper scorn.

"Dass for shoo-er." Kjitel agrees. "Eff yew gice vanna shoot any deerses, yew gotta go vay oop nort."

With that final admonition, Rufus had to bury his head in his beer glass to hide the smile. Chalk up another victory for rural America.

Did you hear the one about the Norwegian who froze to death? He went to the Drive-In Theater to see "Closed for the Season!"

WINTER

Country-School Socials; the End of An Era

The wooden school desks, all mounted on one-by-six planks, were slid tightly together into the corner next to the teacher's massive rolltop desk, the dance floor was now ready.

Only an hour before, parents and kinfolk had struggled valiantly to squeeze hard bodies into those tiny children's seats, there to sit vise-like but still enjoy the situation as they watched their children perform at the monthly Helestad School Community Club.

The performance just finished had been well received. All seventeen kids in the country school took part somehow, someway, doing something. Getting the best laughs and the most applause were two fifth graders, the Lovik cousins, who had dressed in appropriate pig-like costumes and danced around and mimed the words while 78 r.p.m. record player behind the curtain ground out "Who's Afraid of the Big Bad Wolf?"

"Dat vuss a gewd vun," said their Uncle Halvor Lovik, who had watched his nephews clown about in their costumes. "Dey're a couple of sporty fellers, dose two kids are, yew betcha."

Now would follow the best parts of all, the dance, followed by a huge lunch. Back in the alcove entrance Nels Thompson was tuning up his fiddle and beside him stood Peter Strandemoen, strapping on his concertina—or "squeeze-box," as he called it.

A couple of words, a couple of nods, a couple of toe-taps and the band swung into "The Lumberjack Waltz." Immediately the dancers got ready. First to spring forward were Oscar and Florence Arstad, a curious couple partly because he was small and skinny and she was big and fat. But on the dance floor she was as light and nimble and pliable as a ballerina, and as a couple they were marvelous dancers.

Next out came Odvar and Maud Hartvik; Maud in her special dancing dress, new from Sears; Odvar wearing his shiny white shirt matched by equally shiny blue pants. Even his hair shined from a bit too much Brilliantine, the latter adding a competing odor with his wife's Evening in Paris perfume, so much so that Halvor Lovik whispered to his nephews about all the flies coming out and buzzing around Odvar's head.

When the band swung into a schottische, the pairs split off to move into groups of three. That was followed by three fast polkas, every one a foot stomper, every one guaranteed to drive the rats out of any building, and while the feet fell hard in rhythmic patterns, extra hoots and shouts of delight filled the air for the happy dancers.

At last Nels Thompson called the evening's one and only Circle Two Step, and every soul there, except for the new Moen baby who was asleep on the teacher's desk, got into a big circle and joined hands. Grandpa Dahlen had a second grader on one side and the school teacher on the other, but soon they were all mixing partners as Nels shouted directions between fiddle strokes:

"Grandpa Dahlen had a second grader on one side and the school teacher on the other, . . ."

"Ladies on the outside, gents in the middle...and ladies reverse, grab a partner, and EVERYBODY DANCE!" And everybody did dance, following Nels' directions and going whole-hog until Eldred Bestul's final piano chord, a chord which came one beat after the other two bandmembers had stopped.

Community Club Programs. . . new clothes from Sears. . . smelly hair oil drew the flies. . . and the next day was December 7.

Then they all laughed, and Ingeborg Haaverson used that moment to holler: "Lunch time! Line up! Young'uns first, ladies next; you menfolk bring up the rear."

The food took away some of the desire to dance much longer. A couple more turns around the floor was demanded by "Nikolina," however; not to respond to that tune bordered on sacrilege. By that time it was almost 10:30; time to go home and end another glorious Community Club night, despite the thought of all those cows to milk by hand in the morning.

Arne Carlson glanced up to see his daughter trying to slip out the door with a high school boy. HEI DU! (Hey you!) GIT BACK IN HERE! And they got back in there in a hurry, while Arne found it necessary at that moment to inform his wife: "Yew gotta show dose kids who iss boss. Else dey tink dey kin do anyting."

The "god nats" were said by all as the families filed out the door and into the crisp night air of early winter. Out on the front steps came the last ones out, the bandmembers, and they watched as the cars and pickups were starting up and moving in a long line of lights down the driveway, soon to hit the graveled county road and the four corners, there to fan out in all directions for home.

"Y'know," said Nels Thompson, as he tucked his violin case under his arm and pulled on his leather chopper mittens, "dese nights are more blame fun den anything."

"Yah," agreed Eldred Bestul, "Sure iss. Aye did diss as a kid vit my folks; now my kidses are vit me tonight. Y'know, den, Aye hope diss neffer changes. Aye hope diss can go on for anudder hunnert years. Vall, god nat."

The next day was December 7, 1941. The Japanese attacked Pearl Harbor. America—and Helestad School—were never to be the same again.

Everclear and Christmas Cheer

Personal remembrances of earlier times tend to include the pleasant rather than the unpleasant; indeed, the zany events are remembered best of all. Thus, for all those people who lived in this little lutefisk-ghetto at Christmas time, one of their more bizarre recollections was the annual decoration of the outdoor community Christmas tree. This civic project was attempted regularly by the same two volunteers, Knute Hokesvik and Truls Moen, two immigrant Norwegian-American farmers who had since retired and moved to town. The two men seemed to choose the coldest day in December for their decorating, an occasion that became a ritual of yearly entertainment for those who could stay, listen, and witness the debacle, like the following:

9 a.m.

"Hoo hoo! Ve got a purdy spa-ruce tree dis year. Tiss t'irty feet fall if it's an inch. Vell, let's get 'er oop," says Knute Hokesvik.

"Yah-da, den. But dis year ve be more careful and make plumb shoo-er it stands straight. Poosh it a li'l to da nort, Knute. Das it. Yust perfect," replies Truls Moen with certainty as Knute maneuvers the thick trunk into the tree stand. "Nail anudder spike an' it'll be sta-rrrraight foreffer. *Aa, sa fint!* (O so fine.)

"Tiss **Kaldt idag** (cold today). Ay see dat Skol Skogen yust opened da tavern. Brrrrrr. Let's go get a hot punst" (pronounced "poontz"—a popular Norwegian-American winter-drink consisting of a mixture of boiling hot water, a dab of sugar, a touch of lemon, and a couple of jiggers of Everclear, a 190 proof form of grain alcohol).

10 a.m.

"Dere mus' be hunnert yards of beautiful sta-ringed poopcorn here. Uff da. Vell, yew git up on da ladder, Truls, an' Ay'll hand 'em oop. Now be careful and make dose strings hang yust vright. See dere! Dat vun by your leg da-roops tew far. Move it a li'l to da vest. Das it. Das purdy. *Aa sa fint.*"

"Yah, you betcha. Dis'll be da best tree yet, Knute. Da kid-ses vill luff it, and da bird-ses vill come, tew. 'Cept my fingers iss fa-reesing! Let's go git anudder puntz-varmer-upper."

11 a.m.

Uff da, dere must be two hunnert yards of sta-ringed pop-corn. An' you tay me how in da vorld ve fix all dose udder fancy doo-dads up dere hven dey break so easy. Von boomp an' dey bust."

"Vell, ve yust be extry careful, den. C'mon Truls, oop da lad-der."

"Yeepers! But dis ladder iss gettin' shaky. Must be da ice on da bottom. Ve'll hang a few now, an' den let's go over across for sumpin' to steady da nerves. An' besides, tiss **kaldt idag**."

12 noon

"Okday, den. Ve got **mange** (many) tings left to do. Uff da, dere mus' be t'ree hunnert yards of popcorn! Oop on da ladder, Truls."

"**Nei** (No). Yew git up it. Tiss too viggling for me."

"Vell, okay, den. Here goes nuttin'. Hand dat yunk up to me careful-like. Oopsadaisy, yew dropped vun, and it ba-roke into a tousand pieces."

"Ah, who cares?"

"Yeah. Who duss care?"

"**Akurat** (exactly). Hey, Knute, dat vun angel-ting not hang vright. Tiss crooked."

"Ah, who cares?"

"Yeah. who duss care. Le's go git a snort, an' den ve come back an' giff 'er ol' Billy—."

1 p.m.

"Hey dere, stop shakin' da ladder!"

"Ay neffer touched it!"

"Vell, somebody iss makin' it vobble."

"Maybe it's da trolls comin' out from da branches."

"Maybe it's yew tryin' to help me break my neck. **Er du galen**? (Are you crazy?)"

"**Nei**. Hey, le's stop an' git sumpin' to eat. How 'bout a fry-cake (donut) or **fattigmann** (cookie) an' a cuppa Norsk gaso-line?"

"**Nei**, dah. Ve're here to vork, not eat. But maybe anudder nip vould help tings."

2 p.m.

"Uff da, Truls, but dat ba-lame ladder iss dainchrus! Yur turn to crawl oop."

"**NEI!** Ay neffer gittin' up on dat goofy ting."

"Me needer. But how ve git da vrest of da trimmins on da tree? Dere must be four hunnert yards of poop-corn! An how vi git all dis udder stuff on?"

"Simple. Ve'll t'row 'em on. Yust like pitchin' horse-shoes, 'cept straight oop."

"Okay. Here gose a Santa to da top branch. Oops. Missed. But now Ay got 'nudder problem. My neck iss gettin' stiff from all dat lookin' oop."

"Yew tink dat's bad? Ay svallowed my snoose!"

"Aw, **drit**. Le's go haff a punst."

3 p.m.

"Hey! Ay got dat angel to stay up dere purdy good, huh?"

"Yeah. 'Cept da ainch-el iss upside down."

"Ah, who cares?"

"Yah. Who duss care. Dere must be five hunnert yards of dis dumb poopcorn."

"Hey! Ay got dat angel to stay up dere purdy good, huh?"
"Yeah. 'Cept da ainch-el iss upside down."

"Le's stand back furder hven ve t'row da stuff. More shallenge."

"Okay. O hoot-ma-toot! Yew missed da whole tree!"

"Vell, yew ain't no Joe Di-Moch-i-o yurself. But **jeg er trett. Er du?** (I'm tired. Are you?)"

"**Nei**. Yust tirsty. Vun more punst to cut da dust from da road."

"'Cept it's snowin'."

"Vell, dat's close 'nuff."

4 p.m.

"CAREFUL! Truls, yew almos' knock da tree over!"

"HELP HELP! I'M STUCK! GIMME OUT!"

"Vell, kom to tink of it, yew lewk purdy good in dere. Reminds me of seein' a big black bear in da brush-pile. Hoo hoo."

"Ay'll 'hoo hoo' you in da snoot if you don' git me outdahere. HELP!"

"Okay, den. Shush up. Ay help. Das it. Steady. Dere now, yew made it. But shhhhhhhh. Dose gice over dere iss vatching us. Shhhhhhhh."

"Ah, Ay don' giff a hoot. Let 'em lewk."

"Le's stand back, Knute, an' see our bee-oot-ti-fool ta-ree. *Aa sa fint!* Ain't it sumpin'?"

"Cept it's crooked. And dere's a tousan' yards of popcorn hangin' every hvich way."

"Ah, who cares?"

"Yeah, Who duss care."

"Ay tank ay go home. Da missus hass got da supper on, ay s'pose. Vell, *god nat* (good night)."

"Yeah, *god nat*, Truls. *Og Glad Jul* (And Merry Christmas)."

"Truls?"

"Yeah?"

"*Vi har det godt i Amerika.*"

"Yeah, Knute. We do have it good in America."

Coping With Depression Christmas

Generosity, kindness, and love are reflected in Christmas presents from parents to their children. During the Depression years of the 1930's, these parental attributes were still there even when there were no material gifts to give their children. Young people simply lived in the Depression; parents coped with it. The difference was often painful, as this actual event illustrates:

Two boys ran lickety-split across the snowy plowed field, heading kitty-corner across the back forty to save time. The kids aimed tired legs at a sagging farmhouse standing a half-mile in the distance and looking bleak and forlorn under a shelter-belt of scraggy pine and boxelder trees.

"Hey, I gotta slow down. My feet don't always move right in these shoes," said the nine-year-old who was wearing a pair of size 13 army boots. Not that he was complaining because he was actually happy that day, it being the last day of school before Christmas vacation. And it had been his day to go to school, his day to wear the boots. Just stuff the right amount of old newspapers inside them and the same boots would fit all three brothers who had to take turns in the wintertime walking the three miles to country school.

"My Pa's gonna get me a B-B gun for Christmas," he announced to his companion, and the neighbor boy gave a smile of assurance but wondered where the father, Mr. Torkelson, would find any money for such a luxury. Still, Mr. Torkelson was a very nice man. Everybody in the district liked Mr. Torkelson.

"C'mon inside with me and get warmed up when we get there. And maybe Pa will have baked a cake." Again the neighbor boy smiled at his friend's prediction, and again he doubted, for good reason. He had seen his pal's lunches at school, and the menu never varied: homemade brown bread with lard for butter and raw onion pieces between the slices. That was it; that was his total lunch. And yet he heard that Mr. Torkelson did bake pretty well, learning from scratch after his wife died from diptheria three years ago. Mr. Torkelson had learned to do everything on the farm, being both father and mother to his sons. He was a nice man.

The boys bounded up the sagging wooden steps and into the warm kitchen. At the glistening-hot woodstove stood Mr. Torkelson, a massive red-faced man, stirring a steaming kettle. He waved a friendly hello with a wooden spoon, then added: "Hey dere, Ay bet youse gice iss hong-ry. Wanna piece of bread?" That Mr. Torkelson, he was so nice, even though he talked kinda funny.

"What's for supper, Pa?"

"Aye giff yew t'ree guesses, an' da first two don't count."

"What? Oatmeal again? We had that last night and the night before!"

"Vell, den, yew won' die from it. Yet tink of dis pome: 'Close da eyes, open da t'roat, pretend yur eatin' a billy goat.'" His light blue eyes radiated mischief and fun, but the son was not impressed.

"Hey, Pa, I know what I want for a Christmas present." Mr. Torkelson looked quickly down at the bubbling oatmeal.

"Really, Pa. It's the only thing I want this year. Last year I didn't get nothin' for Christmas or my birthday, and next year I don't want nothin' if you'll just buy me a B-B gun. This kid in town will sell his old Daisy air rifle for one dollar. C'mon, Pa, whaddaya say?" Mr. Torkelson didn't say anything. His eyes darkened over.

"Jeepers, Pa. It's Christmas! Buy me a present, just one. Pretty please, Pa. Pretty please with sugar on it."

Mr. Torkelson now looked so sad, and he turned his back on his begging son as though he couldn't stand to hear any more. Then he straightened up quick-like, and instead of talking softly as he usually did, he talked loud, too loud, as though trying to prevent his voice from breaking:

"Diss Ca-riss-muss biss-ness iss yust a racket! Yust dum' adwertice-ing to fool poor folks like uss into spendin' mo-ney we ain't got! Don't yew onnerstand?"

"Ah, heck, Pa. Don't be so tight. Ain't you got no Christmas spirit?"

"Aye got sumpin' for gice like yew who keep on wit smart-alecky vords 'bout press-ents," and he walked over, lifted his arm and back-handed his son on the side of the head, which sent the kid flying headlong into the side of the woodbox. With that the father nervously grabbed a threadbare mackinaw coat and rushed outside, slamming the door behind him.

The neighbor boy looked down in embarrassment. Without glancing at his crying friend, he slid out the door without so much as a goodbye. What's with Mr. Torkelson?

Hurrying across the barnyard and starting to run swiftly for his own farmhome, the neighbor boy stopped suddenly when he heard a strange noise coming from the barn. Moving cautiously, he eased towards the building and knelt down by a small side window, the panes of glass so dirty that the yellow kerosene light from the lantern inside could barely be seen.

The moaning sound kept coming and the boy reached down with his mittened hand and wiped away a circle of dirt on the window. The boy peered through the hole, and then he could make it all out. Then he could see this huge man leaning against the horse stall and crying; he could see the manger sag under the weight of this sobbing hulk whose massive shoulders were convulsing inside an old mackinaw coat. Again and again the figure lunged forward and backward, and finally the big man slid down gently and lay quietly on the dirt floor, his head against the cold white-limed stone wall of the barn. He just lay there, his red-face a picture of sadness and frustration.

The neighbor boy rose to leave, took one more glance, then walked slowly away, at the same time confirming what he always knew: Mr. Torkelson was a very nice man.

Looking For Replacements

Variations on "form letters" remains an on-going way for people to play jokes on each other. The letter below is one Scandinavian version that showed up in several mailboxes, often as Christmas "cards."

Dear_____

Perhaps you have heard of me and my nationwide campaign on the cause of temperance. Each year, for the past 15 years, I have made a tour of Minnesota, Wisconsin, Iowa, North and South Dakota, and have delivered a series of lectures on the evils of drinking.

He sat on the platform picking his nose. . . and making
obscene gestures. . . and would you like to replace him?

On this tour I have been accompanied by my young friend and assistant, Thorvold Lindstrom. Thorvold, a young man of good family and excellent background, was a pathetic example of a life ruined by excessive indulgence in liquor.

Thorvold would appear with me at the lectures and sit on the platform, wheezing and staring at the audience through bleary, bloodshot eyes; he would also be sweating profusely, picking his nose, scratching his crotch, passing gas, and making obscene gestures, while I at the same time would point to Thorvold as an example of what overindulgence can do to a person.

Unfortunately, Thorvold recently passed away, his liver having at last given out.

A mutual acquaintance of ours has given me your name, and I wonder if you would be available to take Thorvold's place on my lecture tour this spring?

> Yours in Hope,
> Ingebret Bjornson

How Not to Collect Money for the Pastor

When it came to consuming alcohol, the menfolk on the farms in Glenwood township were moderate drinkers indeed. In the country home of Lars Lee, my grandfather, there was just one small bottle of liquor, a pint of Everclear alcohol which sat on the top shelf in the kitchen cabinet, right beside the bottles of Karo syrup and Watkin's vanilla. This liquor would last Lars Lee at least a year or more.

Everclear was strong stuff, 190 proof to be exact, thus almost pure alcohol. It was used mainly as a form of medicine in a mixed concoction called simply "puntz" (poontz). A shot or two of Everclear was poured into a cup of boiling hot water, and to this combination came a teaspoon of sugar, and sometimes a **tich** of cinnamon. Hot puntz was primarily taken for colds—or to prevent colds from occurring—but on special occasion some farm folks might serve puntz to guests for social reasons, but the emphasis was on **one** puntz only, given the power that lay in just one drink.

Lars Lee (as my father, at age 89, told it) was a moderate drinker. Intoxication was to be avoided above all considerations; men could drink providing they never allowed themselves to get drunk.

So it was always sobriety for Lars Lee, except for one solitary time when he inadvertently got totally bombed on a Christmas Eve day, and it all happened for an on a good and noble cause.

Salaries for rural Lutheran ministers during the first half of the twentieth century were low. At times the pay amounted to a pittance, and it was often hand-to-mouth living for families of the **prest** (priest/pastor). Their rewards were presumably to come later; in the meantime, here on earth, the pastors made do with the little money they received for their efforts.

Worldly gifts for the Glenwood pastor came only once during the year, at Christmas when a special donation of money was presented to the pastor and his family at Christmas Eve services.

This special fund-for-the-pastor was collected on Christmas Eve day each year by someone designated to do so by the Board of Deacons, and this someone designated this one year was Lars Lee. On the surface he was a good choice.

Lars was an immigrant from Laerdahl, Norway, arriving in America in 1878 at the age of 22. He first tried homesteading in northwestern North Dakota, but after two years of living in a sod-hut, he abandoned that land, blaming the alkali water as much as anything for his decision to move to Decorah, Iowa, and buy a small farm there which an older brother had originally owned.

The best of intentions can lead to. . . the worst of conditions—and drunken grandfathers—and chaotic sleigh-rides—and rescues by the Lord, or at least from the wife.

Lars Lee was physically a big man, standing over six feet tall and "strong as an ox," as my father described him. Lars wore a large walrus moustache, and he smoked a half dozen different pipes which he always filled with Prince Albert tobacco. (This habit was testified to later by the hundreds if not thousands of empty tobacco cans lying over the entire length and breadth of his eighty-five acre farmstead.)

Anyway, Lars agreed to collect **penger for presten** (money for the pastor). So, on this bitter cold Christmas Eve day, Lars hitched up one of his two horses to a small sleigh as soon as he had finished the morning chores. The snowstorm of the previous day had ended, leaving an excellent sleighing surface which permitted his going cross-country as well as following the primitive roads.

His mission was clear and simple and honorable: he was to travel to all the farm homes within a four mile radius and accept the donations. He told his wife that he would be home by early afternoon, "Og vaer ikke redd" (and not to worry).

His problem started early, compounded by the cold weather and the spirit of Christmas-giving, which is to say that at every farm house at which he stopped, the owners insisted that Lars come into the kitchen to warm up a bit—and have just one hot puntz to ward off the icy chill.

In these farmyard encounters, all conducted in Norwegian, of course, he was to hear the same two lines over and over again:

"Det er fryktelig kaldt idag." (It is so terribly cold today.)

"Du maa jo ha en puntz, da." (You must have a puntz, then.)

Even by 10 a.m. the effects of his benefactors' gifts were evident as his speech was getting slurred; by 11 a.m. he was wobbling as he walked; by noon he was singing Christmas carols at the top of his voice; by one o'clock the sleigh was making erratic circles in the snow; by two p.m. he could no longer get out of the sleigh; by three he could not even talk clearly enough to explain his drunken appearance in farmyards; he just mumbled some gibberish, after which he held out a small sack, expecting magic results.

At four o'clock the winter sun was getting low in the horizon, and Lars' wife sat by the window, gazing with wonder and apprehension at the long mile-driveway leading up to the main road. Where was Pa?

At 4:30 she spied the horse and sleigh coming down the driveway, but still having anxieties, she rushed out the door, there to find the sweating horse standing quietly in front of the barnyard gate, the sleigh empty of any occupant.

What happened? Where was he? She ran into the house to fetch some warm clothes, then ran out again, got into the sleigh and turned the weary horse around and hurriedly began retracing the route, following the old trails in the fresh snow.

About a mile from home she could first hear this voice hollering hoarsely and somewhat feebly from the corner of the section line: "Hjelp! Hjelp meg!" (Help me!) "Herre Gud! (Lord God) Hjelp!"

The horse, sleigh and wife rushed towards the mournful sounds, and when they got to the fence line they saw Lars Lee lying in the snow, wrapped up and wrestling with a barbed wire fence, and crying out his predicament: "Herre Gud! Naa er jeg visst blitt tatt av djevelen, og kan ikke faa meg vekk." (God, I'm stuck! The devil must have me!)

After much pushing and shoving and wire-bending—and several lines of wifely editorial comment—the woman got her husband untangled from the barbed-wire, and with a final burst of her energy, hoisted her big hulk of a husband into the back of the sleigh.

Before Lars passed out under the buffalo-robe that the wife had covered him with, he had one final message to the deity:

"Naa er jeg all right. Jeg trenger ikke hjelpen din noe mere." (I'm all right now. I don't need your help any more.)

Epilogue: Luckily the money-sack was in the pocket of Lars' mackinaw coat, and so the preacher did get this special fund that Christmas Eve. It was not so strange, however, that the Board of Deacons chose someone else the following year to do the collecting.

Surprises for All At
The Boresville Cafe

The sagging, nondescript corner restaurant—with the aroma of overcooked cabbage from the noon-hour-special still hanging heavily in the air—had only one booth of customers, some giggling high school kids.

The kids were less customers than squatters seeking a warm place to congregate away from home, a communal spot to shoot the breeze and waste away another dull night in what they regarded as their deadingly dull town. Maybe next week would be better, they hoped, as Christmas vacation would be starting.

The kids were practicing basketball cheers, including a new one—a few simple, corny lines stolen from an out of state high school via a letter from a cousin. The letter's recipient was, at the moment, trying to teach her peers, who were not cooperative: "C'mon, you finks, it's easy, and it's Ritzy, too. It goes like this:

'The Lambeth Walk and the Susy-Q, C'mon, Boys, Let's Truck on Through!' "

At the counter sat Halvard Blekken, the fat cafe owner, who was unimpressed by both the dumb lines and the shrieking laughter that followed from the raucous crew in the corner. He suffered the noise nightly. But after all, he had told himself so many times, he could put up with the semi-rowdy kids because he could agree with them that there was really nothing much for kids to do in town. So as long as they bought a Coke or a Pepsi now and then—and it was mainly then—Halvard let them hang out there till the 9:30 closing hour, a time fast-approaching, according to his pocket watch. Those kids could make a nickel bottle of 12-ounce Pepsi last a nighttime.

Halvard looked outside at a lousy, biting cold winter night and saw a land of no-necked people, persons whose necks disappeared from November to March as they pulled heads deep down into their collars. Just another nothing-kind of winter night in this nothing-town where nothing ever happened. Maybe the kids' name for the town was right: Boresville, USA, Unincorporated. And Christmas coming soon, too. Well, reasoned Halvard, there was no Christmas spirit in this jerk-water-four-corners, and any weirdo who said Merry Christmas ought to have his fool head examined.

The cafe door opened suddenly and filing in from the frigid air were the very familiar Oskar Gunderson, and behind him a very unfamiliar family of five, the parents and three small children, including a crying baby carried on the hip of the mother.

While old Oskar settled into his usual swivel stool at the counter, the family skittered to a booth to shed their coats, scarves and mittens and within seconds they all made a bee-line for the lavatories, with the skinny father whispering nervously to the retreating wife:

"I tell you we **don't** have the dough to be in here," but the wife tried to ignore him as she herded shuffling, whining toddlers ahead of her to the toilets.

Oskar, now pulling out a black, stubby, stinking pipe, watched the parade and heard the man's frantic plea, with Oskar apparently deciding that the manner and speed with which they headed for the bathrooms was sufficient reason to stop. Striking a wooden match along the side of his trousers, Oskar lit the smelly pipe and simultaneously ordered his usual **gjetost** (goat cheese), crackers, fry-cakes (donuts) and coffee. Oskar looked like a hobo who belonged at the depot bumshack.

And the high school kids watched Oskar, the man who to them was dirty, gruff, and crusty, with the bark still on him. A Norwegian mountain-man. To the kids he was an old fossil, a tight-lipped, tight-wadded bachelor farmer who with his brother Tobias—and his sister Synove to do the housework—still farmed a quarter section of land with horses in that area south of town called Dane Valley. The kids called him "Odious Oskar," behind his back, and sometimes "Odiferous Oskar," depending on his smell that day. They regarded him as an ancient skinflint who must hate people. And dogs. And fun. And wasn't he always complaining? Why Halvard himself had told the kids that if Oskar was ever hanged, he'd complain if it wasn't a new rope being used. Then too Oskar talked so goofy, and he looked so awful, so "farmerish." Ish da.

One thing about Oskar's appearance and dress, it was always the same: shabby. And he invariably wore the same amount of clothes whether winter or summer: He wore long underwear, be it August or January; always two pairs of pants—the inner pair held up with faded green suspenders—and the other pair were bib overalls. Along with two pants were two shirts, the inner one flannel and the outer one wool. And this night, because he was apparently trying to fight off a sore throat, he had a wool sock wrapped around his long turkey-neck, the sock soaked in Mentholatum. This night he was Odiferous Oskar. Yuk, said the high school kids, the likes of him should be locked in the coal bin of the Old People's Home.

Back to their booth came the family, all looking obviously tired and the father obviously frazzled and worried. Once again he whispered about money to his busy wife who was trying to wipe noses and dry hands: "I tell you we ain't likely got enough to make it on—and for sure if we order to much too eat. Don't order big!"

"But we're all so hungry," pleaded the thin-looking, cold-looking young wife. "The children haven't hardly had a thing since we left at dawn," and she picked up the plastic-coated menu and hid her face behind it trying to avoid further arguing or conflict. Halvard the proprieter wasn't exactly enjoying the scene either for lots of reasons, including the fact that he would make no money off this outfit.

The high school kids peeked around their booth corner and looked at the worried Halvard who was now looking at the disreputable Oskar who in turn was observing the strangers. Strangers in town sure stand out; people just don't look at them, they stare at them, and Oskar was staring. "How uncouth," said one adolescent to her friend. "Oskar is a pathetic jerk." "Yah," agreed the friend with a laugh: "How 'uncoot' of that old coot," and they giggled again as Halvard, with pad and pencil, lumbered over to the far booth and said in his most practiced, casual manner: "You folks decided what you want to eat?"

To Halvard's request came a squeaky voice from a tow-headed little boy: "Yup. I want to order half a hamburger," to which line Halvard chuckled and the high school kids had a silent laughing-fit over, and even Oskar had to smile at the little guy.

"No," said the mother quietly but firmly, "we all must eat something nourishing, food that 'will stick to the ribs," as Grandma says. By the way, we've still a hundred miles to go before we get to Gram's house. Anyway, we will order four regular roastbeef dinners with mashed potatoes and gravy and green beans. And milk for everyone."

The hollow-cheeked husband let out an audible groan but recovered to emit a half-cry: "I don't think we've got enough to cover it," and the wife sounded fearful herself in answering: "I have some change at the bottom of my purse. We'll make it somehow."

"Geez, I don't know how," he replied sadly. "An' we gotta get gas yet; too. And I think my credit-card might be over-extended. O boy, O brother; it's the poor farm for us. Some kind of 'merry Christmas' this will be if we get stranded and can't make it to your folks' place," and he tapped the tabletop with figeting, bony fingers. The poor guy looked like he lost his last friend.

Oskar kept peeking around and listening to the unhappy couple. Meanwhile he dunked his donuts into his coffee cup but drank—rather slurped—the hot coffee from a saucer, a sight that made the high school kids crinkle up their noses, roll their eyes heavenward, and turn away. These disgusting old people. Oskar, your social pilot-light burns low.

Halvard at last came out from the kitchen with their food and set the plates down before the family members, but before a fork was raised, the family bowed their heads while the father murmured a short prayer, after which they dived into the food with speed caused by near famishment.

Oskar kept glancing at the eating family and a big smile came to his black-whiskered face as he watched the red-haired infant in the high chair half-swallowing, half-spitting the potatoes that the mother was trying so patiently to get into the child's mouth. Soon there were more mashed potatoes in the child's hair than on the plate, and green beans were flying everywhere.

The little guy who had ordered half-hamburger pounded the end of the ketchup bottle trying to get some out, and it came out all right, came out all at once in large quantities all over his plate and the mother's plate and much of the table top. The mother never got flustered, never raised her voice as she carefully wiped up the mess while simultaneously giving advice to the boys, feeding the baby and herself at the same time.

Some thirty seconds after grace ended, the father had scarfed up his plate of food so fast that it appeared he had inhaled it all in one breath. He then pursued the beans that the baby was flinging. To this scene the high school kids sniggered; Halvard shook his head in wonderment; Oskar turned back and took another slurp of coffee, but it appeared that he was bothered by something.

The dreaded moment came when the hulking Halvard waddled over to their booth and laid the bill on the edge of the table, said his usual "Thanks, folks," and lumbered away again. Even Halvard appeared to wonder if he would get paid because he thought he had seen the husband's face turn a little white when he flipped over the slip and saw the total amount of the bill. The show-down was fast-approaching.

Oskar, back at the counter, his coffee and donuts finished, was trying to raise his arthritic body off the stool, and he slowly made it to a standing position. He scooped up his own check and reached for a warped billfold in the ripped top pocket of his overalls. Then Oskar did something else. He sidled over to the family's booth and stood there a few seconds, shuffling from one leg to another, while picking his tobacco-stained teeth with a matchstick. Oskar's disheveled, grizzled appearance would have scared anybody who didn't know him, but before the family members could react in any way, Oskar said:

"Lemme git dis. Yew folks need it," and a gnarled, dirty hand whisked away the slip lying there. Next Oskar pulled a twenty-dollar bill from his soiled wallet and laid it gently on the father's empty plate. "Here, den, take dis, tew. 'Tiss a Ca-riss-miss prrress-int," mumbled Oskar, who turned to leave, then turned back again:

"Vatchin' dose kidses eat wuss mur fun den listenin' to ten Yak Benny radio showsss." Rather quickly Oskar moved back to the counter, laid the checks and some money on the glass show-case counter, tightened the wool sock around his angular neck, threw on a tattered, threadbare denim barn-coat and a black cap, and as he hunkered his head down into the upturned collar, he turned back to the startled family in the booth: "Yah-da, den, Merry Ca-riss-miss," he said, and he shuffled out the door and into the darkness of the winter night.

The high school kids looked back and forth at each other in disbelief; Halvard's eyes just widened bit and seemed to stay that way; the mother and the father glanced at each other, but neither could talk. Finally the one little guy broke the silence: "My, but he was a nice man." Still the parents could say nothing. Then up squeaked the other little boy: "Somebody should have wished him a Merry Christmas, too."

"I think, dear," said the mother very softly, "that somehow he already knows."

Misperceiving
'The American Dream'

Everybody loved Buddy Peterson, and Buddy seemed to love everybody. Buddy was fun to have around and to be around as he was so genuinely nice to everybody.

And Buddy Peterson was a worker. Oh, how he loved to work—and work fast—and work all day and half the night. Folks returning home at midnight from the second movie-showing would see those Allis-Chalmer tractor lights bumping and bobbing in the fields, and they'd smile and say: "There's Buddy Peterson at it again! Wotta worker!"

Work hard, play hard, have fun! That was his motto. And hurry up! 'cause the work has to be done by yesterday! He was born with bib-overalls on, said the men who gathered to talk on main street, all duly impressed by Buddy both as a personality and a devotee of the work ethic.

Buddy set the records for effort. When the winter snows first began to melt on those warm March days, who would be the very first farmer out with the manure spreader? Buddy Peterson, of course. He was admired as much as he was admirable; he just oozed verve and activity and happiness.

His real name was William, but not one citizen in a hundred could come up with his given name. It was always Buddy, or Bud, the only son of a prominent, civic-minded dairy farmer whose small farm was within the village limits. Physically Buddy was short and stocky, and there always seemed to be a perpetual smile on his face and a twinkle in his dancing blue eyes. He simply radiated warmth and charm and goodness.

After attending eight grades of grammar school, Buddy went straight into fulltime farming with his Dad. He didn't have time to waste sitting still in a high school because there was too much to be done on the farm, and Buddy had too much energy just to sit with a book in his hands.

Bud was a young man on the run. Literally. He ran from the house to the barn, from the barn to the machine shed, from the shed to his little shack where he slept during the summer. Driving his Dad's milk route before dawn, he would sometimes push the truck gears into "gramma low," then set the steering wheel to go straight, and then he'd run back and forth from the moving, driverless truck, delivering Peterson's Dairy Milk, the kind where the thick cream rose to the top one-third of the glass quart-jars.

Even a short stint in the U.S. Army in World War II didn't slow him down. He enlisted on January 16, 1945, and served as a gunner with the 316th Field Artillery Battalion in the Asiatic Theater of Operations. He returned to the states in December of 1945 and was honorably discharged as a Technician 4th Grade on April 4, 1946.

When Buddy returned to the farm, he seemed to work even harder, doing routine jobs in such a special way as to make the whole community notice. For example, his hay loads were the highest and widest in the area, sometimes to the displeasure of his father because the loads were often too big to go through the barn door to the hay loft, so they would have to partially unload the hay by hand before they could get it in to use the regular unloading fork.

Bud's hay loads frequently stopped the traffic on the highway between the field and the driveway to the farm, but the drivers of that day in that community never expressed displeasure or inconvenience as they were awed by what they saw on the horse-driven wagon. Not incidentally, the Peterson horses always had plenty of tender loving care and were not abused or misused; even the horses seemed to sense the pride of the driver and the loads of hay they were pulling.

It wasn't all work. At the Saturday night old-time dances at the Community Hall, the girls liked to dance with Buddy, because he really moved fast on the floor. He'd dance, perspire, dance some more, then sweat some more, then wipe the sweat from his high forehead and wet head, then fly back to the dance floor until that final one o'clock polka brought the dancing to a close. And then he'd run across the street to get a couple of snorts before the taverns closed—and then home, and after a couple of hours of sleep, he'd bounce out of bed before sunrise to start another wonderful day.

Buddy was a young man on the move, all right, and a joy to follow, if one could catch up with him. Ladies standing with their shopping bags in front of the grocery store would turn their heads and smile with pleasure and amusement as Buddy, still a bachelor, whirled by them and on down the sidewalk: "Yah, that Buddy Peterson is one swell guy. Too bad our girls didn't marry the likes of him."

The area high school kids thought he was a great guy, too. While other Luther Leaguers in the neighboring towns had to resort to using tractors to pull their sleighs for their Sunday night hay-ride parties, the locals got Buddy Peterson because he'd have the real thing—horses! And he'd have that sleigh shined up and have at least three feet of hay on the rack for the kids to bury into on frigid nights.

Best of all on these hayrides, Buddy would be along to drive and at the same time bring an air of festivity for all the rest of the group to catch. Sometimes Bud would hand someone else the reins and then he'd run along beside the sleigh and grab the legs of some couple under the hay and he'd pull the smoochers off and toss them good naturedly into a snow bank. Then he'd laugh, and the couple would laugh, and the whole sleigh-full of people would laugh.

Even the little kids in town loved Buddy. He'd grab them and throw them up in the air and pretend to drop them when they came sailing down—and then he'd laugh, and the kids would laugh, and the moms, too, joined in the fun created by Buddy Peterson.

Buddy enjoyed making people laugh. Who else would dress up like a woman—with big balloons stuffed in for a huge bust—and run along beside the high school band during the Community Fair Parade and mock-scare the ladies and men along the sidewalks by pretending that he was going to kiss them.

At one Fair he decided that the entertainment planned was insufficient. The Fair needed some more local color than just rides, concession-stands, and the like; the Fair needed some excitement—like someone jumping from a plane in a parachute (namely himself) even if that person had never made a parachute-jump in his life! So Buddy sent away for a parachute, read up on the procedure on how-to-do-it, and conned a friend into taking him up in his plane. And he jumped! He landed in a tree some distance from his planned target, and as he was coming down he called out: "I'm having the best time of my life!"

(This incident was not told to his family beforehand as his mother was ill at the time and anticipating major surgery. Bud was very close to his mother and did not want her to worry about him.)

This parachute-business was typical Buddy Peterson; it was daring, exciting and fun. Whenever he came bouncing into a circle of people, his bandy-legs on springs, the faces of all the folks just lit up with smiles because just his presence meant fun.

Chuckles and laughs and good fellowship and kindness exuded from Buddy Peterson. He became the symbol in the community for liveliness and pleasure; he was the bright star whose warm, outgoing personality twinkled constantly for his many admirers. He appeared to be a perfect role-model. He seemed to be the happiest, the most likeable young man in town, the one whose future seemed a guarantee of success. The American Dream was personified in this wonderful, handsome lad.

Everybody loved Buddy Peterson, but apparently Buddy did not love everybody or at least everything. On December 27, 1950, William (Buddy) Peterson, age 31, went out to his black sedan behind the dairy store, put his old 30-30 deer rifle to his heart and killed himself.

O Lord, Deliver Me From the Annual Church Meeting

Parishioners who suffer through those insufferably long, annual, January church meetings are people who fall into a special category for patience, if not always piety. Perhaps even more deadly-dull than the meetings are the minutes-of-the-meeting itself, those bone-dry documents read only by the secretary before filed away in some dusty drawer, never to be viewed again. It is that kind of church-meeting—and that kind of secretary's minutes—that leads to conjuration about. . .

The Minutes of the Annual Meeting of
THE CHURCH OF LUTHERAN CONFUSION

The meeting was scheduled to begin at 8 p.m., but was delayed in the absence of President Olaf Stutterson. The Secretary, Telford Scriben, stated that he had observed the President entering the Happy Norteman Bar across the street at 7:30. At 8:05 the Church Council was sent to summon the President to the meeting. At 8:30 the Board of Education was sent to summon the Church Council. Finally, at 8:45, President Stutterson

declared the meeting in session and being somewhat disoriented, brought down the gavel on Secretary Scriben's hand,
making him unable to write. The President then glibly commented that since Scriben had been Secretary for 37 years, he
would probably enjoy a break. After this bad joke was explained to the two Swedes at the meeting, the group got down
to business.

The pastor, the Rev. Gunnar Pleasdemall, opened the
meeting with a prayer, and afterwards the President thanked
him and noted that the prayer was typical of the Reverend in
that it was too long.

Next a new member of the congregation was voted in, Charlie
Joiner, and the President expressed surprise that Joiner was
wearing a hearing aid. Joiner assured him that it was only an
ear-plug to his transistor radio in his pocket; he didn't want to
miss the ballgame.

The Treasurer, Odvar Loanshark, gave the congregational
financial report which, according to his questionable figures,
showed a balance of $1.98 for the year. After minor grumbling
about an audit-one-of-these-years, the report was accepted by a
close vote.

Then the chairman of the Board of Operations, Artur Simple,
reported that all the property was in good working order, except
that the church needed a new riding lawn-mower for the lazy
custodian. Chairman Simple said that if his board was only
given more power, they could purchase the mower from his
brother-in-law's hardware store for the small sum of $3,398.00.
When spending was mentioned, Percy Pinchpenny woke up to
ask where in thunderation the money was going to come from?
Simple explained that they would borrow it from the Ladies
Aid, the aid having a checking account of $99,000.00, and the
Aid president said that the congregation could borrow money
from their special living-perpetual-bake-sale fund. The Ladies
Aid President, Agnes Scrimp, agreed that they would be proud
to furnish the money for the mower—at 24 per cent interest.

A motion carried, sort of, to buy the mower. At this point the
President called for order as a fight broke out among the Coun-

cil members as to who would get to ride the lawn mower first.

The next report came from the Superintendent of the Sunday School, Johannes Klunk. Klunk stated that the school year was going along just hunky-dory, but he did want to clarify a few reports circulating about the Sunday School kids. It's true, he said, that all the hubcaps had been taken from the pastor's car. But there was an explanation. The three students who took the hubcaps were admonished under the Discipline Rule of Matthew 18:15-18. The boys confessed that they did not know it was the pastor's car, or else they would have taken only two of them.

Then Gladyce Goodbody, chairman of the town's Prudery Club, rose to object to the new sex-education series being used in the classes. "It's just a shame," she said, "telling youth that there are differences between males and females." The Superintendent was then asked to defend himself against her charge. "Actually," replied the super, "I'm not sure just what the children are learning, but the teachers are certainly acting differently. They seem to smile a lot more, and they have a twinkle in their eyes."

The church Evangelism Board chairman, Ben Brassy, reported next. He said that the new Evangelism program entitled "Sure-Shooters for Salvation" had begun. Basically the program consisted of each evangelist being armed with a toy pistol which fired a hard plastic bullet with a Bible verse written on the bullet; also provocative theological questions were written on tiny slips of paper stuffed inside the bullets. The plan did have a couple of drawbacks, he admitted. Three of his evangelism-callers had been fired back at with live ammunition; two others had been confronted by a karate expert, and one of them had been chased by a German Shepherd owned by a Finnlander who mistook him for a Catholic.

Chairman Brassy also asked if they would be interested in hearing some questions that his callers had asked congregational members. President Stutterson said no, they wouldn't, but Brassy told them anyway. Ten persons were asked: "If you died tonight, where would you want to spend eternity?" Three answered Minneapolis; five replied Las Vegas; two said Acupulco, and two spinsters replied they wanted to go to Hell, Michigan.

The next report was from Paul Pounder, the church organist. He reported that certain troubles in the liturgy of the new contemporary worship service had not worked out. Thus, in consultation with the pastor and the Board of Music, it was decided to keep on saying "Hallelujah" after the Epistle reading, rather than shouting "Right on!" Also the spoken "Amen" will be retained after the prayers instead of saying "You bet your sweet bippy!"

Next came a report from the Special Effects sub-committee of the Vestibule Committee with the spokesman apologizing for the confusion caused at the last Ascension Day Service. While they thought it was a good idea to rig a harness under the pastor's vestments and raise him 35 feet into the air as he gave the final benediction, they had no idea of the number of people in church with heart conditions. Nor did they consider that the rope might break. The chairman then thanked the pastor for trying the stunt, and he noted how pleased he was to see the pastor out of traction.

Finally, Pastor Pleasdemall gave his annual report, and his report was accepted, grudgingly. Among the minor things said by the pastor was his comment on the recent arrival to the community of the new minister of the Unitarian Church. The pastor noted that while it was true that they were forming a group in the Lutheran Church to study other religions, he thought it unfortunate that some members took it upon themselves to burn a question mark on the lawn of the new minister. He said such action in the future should be cleared first with the Board of Fellowship.

Someone then spoke up to say that Oscar Sham no longer came to church and wondered why. Pres. Stutterson suggested it might be because of the incident at the mortgage-burning-ceremony for the Education Unit last summer when Oscar held on to the flaming papers too long and burned his fingers. That caused Oscar to drop the burning mortgage on the floor which set the whole church on fire. A motion then carried to send a letter of praise to the town fire department for responding so quickly, but an amendment was added asking if they really had to chop down the front doors just for practice? The President also noted that while Oscar was in the hospital, it probably wasn't in good taste for the pastor in his visit to refer to Oscar as "Butterfingers."

At the close of the meeting Ralph Smiley, the local Lutheran Brotherhood Insurance Company peddler, showed an old filmstrip entitled "Keep Them Alive Till '85," after which he handed out some useless calendars. But to the womenfolk, Smiley gave a recipe for Elephant Stew which he said would be a great contribution in preparing for Congregational Picnics. Mrs. Rufus (Fertile Myrtle) Johnson, mother of 17, said she wanted the recipe in the minutes so that all the elephant hunters in the church could use it:

"Ingredients—one large elephant, seasoned with brown gravy, and two rabbits (the rabbits are optional, however). Cut the meat into bite-size pieces; this should take about two months, and it will provide the Luther League kids with something to do to keep them out of the bowling alleys. Next, cover with gravy and cook on a kerosene stove at 500 degrees temperature for about three weeks. Then serve. This recipe will serve about 1800 confirmed members. If more are expected for the meal, add the two rabbits. Do this only if necessary as most people don't like to find hares in their food."

There being no other proper or improper business to be brought before the body, the annual meeting of the Church of Lutheran Confusion was declared adjourned.

Grounds For Divorce. . . Norwegian Styles (?) #I

She was a very nice youngish married lady who tried to be even nicer to make up for her mercurial husband who could be absolutely wicked—and yet positively charming at times. This quixotic mate was a kind of Dr. Jeckyl-son, Mr. Hyde-son. When he was good, he was very very good, but when he was bad he was. . .a real jerk.

The husband in his waspish moments would say either the wrong thing at the right time, or vice versa; whichever way said, his words would invariably embarrass, yea mortify his wife.

Such was the situation this one evening when the wife was holding a fancy dinner-gathering at her home, a planned special-meal for special guests who were notable figures in the community. Small scale notables, maybe, but nevertheless she did want to impress favorably those gathered at her sumptuous table, and so she made extra efforts to be a superb hostess, a super cook, and a charming conversationalist.

By the time the dessert was served and the final coffee consumed, the wife had accomplished all three of her goals. It had been a charming evening. Her husband, as he had oh-so-faithfully promised, had held his tart tongue and behaved in a most civilized manner. He conducted himself with deportment and guarded his words, if not his thoughts. Would that this guarding have lasted.

The well-dressed, well-mannered guests sat around the large dining room table. Full and presumably happy, they all chatted amiably, saying all those right words that mark social etiquette which in total conversation meant little or nothing but was nevertheless important to the tone of the gathering. It was all so polite and proper, the way the hostess dreamed it might be.

Then somehow the conversational topic steered into the number of years the lovely hostess had been married, and she cheerfully answered "Fifteen."

"No, dear," replied the husband, apparently correcting her, "it's seventeen years."

"Why dear," she replied in a semi-surprised voice, "of course it's fifteen. I remember our marriage date distinctly," and she went on to state the month, day, year and even the hour of their matrimonial vows, vows about to become unglued.

"But dear," responded the husband, prepared to lay on the

evening's show-stopper, "you've got to remember that we started two years earlier."

#II

She was a very sweet oldish married lady who tried to be even sweeter to her husband. She was too sweet for him and everybody else, too. She was so sickly, icky, yukkety sweet as to give all people near her a case of diabetes.

Mrs. Maren Norum was always smiling, actually beaming with a fixed radiant smile that bordered on the moronic. And when she spoke, she always talked in CAPITAL LETTERS, enunciating each word carefully, spitting out every syllable through her tightly-fitting false teeth. (People knew they were false because she smiled so widely that the top of her plate showed.)

Her smiling sentences in CAPITAL LETTERS came out as syrupy epigrams, lines of banalities that from her were supposed to sound like supersophisticated profundities. Sample: "ONE TODAY IS WORTH TWO TOMORROWS."

Her mental burdens seemed to come primarily in inconsequential commitments made daily. Sample: should she go to the store for a loaf of bread of stay home and write another sonnet to Pitty-Pat, her tiny mongrel dog, a pampered pooch whose collar was decorated daily with a freshly washed and ironed ribbon tied into a bow.

Even the dog was sickly sweet. If Pitty-Pat were to bite anyone, the person would never get rabies, just a burst of sugar-energy in the wound.

While all of the local people worried about the outcome of World War II, Mrs. Norum worried about enough water for the bird-bath; while her estranged neighbors discussed the Ardennes Forest Campaign in Europe, Mrs. Norum talked to her flowers about universal-love; while poor Mr. Norum worked overtime to make ends meet, Mrs. Norum fed warm milk to all the stray cats in the county. Mrs. Norum suffered from terminal niceness.

Everyone felt sorry for Mr. Norum, no one felt sorry for Mrs.

Grounds for Divorce. . . .

Mr. Rømegrøt: "That Ingwald is such a braggert. He claims that he's gone out with every middle-aged woman in town, except for one!"

Mrs. Rømegrøt: "Humph! I'll bet it's that snooty Mrs. Ertresvaag on Second Street!"

Norum. Whatever she had—was it a disease?—they hoped it wasn't catching. People would walk across the street to avoid her if they saw her coming at them from a distance. (Who wanted to be stopped in the middle of the sidewalk to hear, in iambic pentameter, Mrs. Norum's latest paean to Pitty-Pat?)

Poor Mr. Norum. He couldn't go to the local summer ballgames: "SUNDAY IS A DAY OF REST." He couldn't go to the local taverns: "SALOONS ARE DENS OF INIQUITY." He was not allowed to sit idly in a chair at home and do nothing; he just couldn't sit there loafing: "IDLE HANDS ARE THE DEVIL'S WORKSHOP." He could not stay up beyond ten o'clock: "EARLY TO BED AND EARLY TO RISE MAKES A MAN HEALTHY, WEALTHY AND WISE." When Mrs. Norum spoke to Mr. Norum in CAPITAL LETTERS, he listened, he responded, he minded—and then one day he did something else.

On a routine Monday morning, Mr. Norum routinely walked out the front door of the house to go to work; he took his regular black lunch pail, wore his regular work-clothes, said his regular goodbye, received his regular sweet smile along with his regular reminder: "FAREWELL, SWEETNESS; AND REMEMBER, DRIVE CAREFULLY."

Mr. Norum drove carefully away, but he never came back home that night, nor the next night, nor ever. The car was found several days later at an airport twenty-five miles away. Mr. Norum disappeared, sort of; Mrs. Norum never heard from him again.

The Case of the Missing Car Tires: Unplanned Manslaughter Perhaps Justifiable

World War II was going great on both battle fronts; American G.I.'s were making rapid advancements towards victory. Back on the home front, however, things were not going great for Thorlief Egli who was making a rapid retreat towards collapse, all because of some car tires.

Thorlief had already made two trips to the county office of the OPA (Office of Price Administration), wasting both precious tires and gasoline to get there. And for nothing. That OPA man—"confounded infernal Swede," Thorlief called him—would not issue Thorlief a mandatory gas-ration-coupon-book until Thorlief turned in some extra tires that he had been hoarding.

Hoarding during the war was popular but unpatriotic. "Don't you know there's a war on?" said that smart-aleck OPA man to Thorlief. Of course he knew, that dumb-cluck! He also knew he didn't want to give up any tires.

When gas-rationing started, each car owner seeking a coupon-book was allowed to have five tires. Thorlief Egli had nine tires. And oh my and uff da but tires were special! Tires were the first product to be rationed just twenty days after Pearl Harbor, so to buy new tires after this was impossible. Now gas was being rationed, too, to two gallons a week, and any car owner had to have that ration-book to purchase those two measely gallons.

As that lunk-head OPA man explained it to Thorlief, the situation was simple: no tires, no gas. So you must turn in those extras! Yet it just about killed Thorlief to have to give up four perfectly good and useable Goodyears, each "wit' a t'ousan' miles left on 'em, den," he whined. He'd much rather trade in his mother-in-law to the OPA, but nope, it had to be his beloved tires. It hurt so bad that he wanted to cry. Yet if he wanted to drive at all, he had to have the coupon-gas-stamps. That situation was simple, too: no stamps, no gas. So good-bye to those extra tires.

On the morning of this special day in his life, Thorlief blocked up his aging De Soto and removed the wheels. Then he took off each tire from the rim and inspected thoroughly, inch by inch, all of his nine tires, agonizing continually over the decision of which to keep and which to turn in to the OPA.

Finally by noon he finished. The five tires he decided to keep

"Poor Thorlief. He'd much rather trade in his mother-in-law. . . but nope, it had to be his beloved tires."

he rolled over alongside his garage with the plans to put them back on the car that night. As already planned, he called his neighbor: " 'ello, den ssCharlie, is yew ready, den?" And as arranged, Charlie came to pick up Thorlief and the four tires as Charlie was going to the OPA anyway.

And off they went on their sad trip. Poor Thorlief. It was a sad journey, all right. That morning he had nine precious tires; by noon he was down to five; by night he would be down to zero.

Thorlief Egli's house stood on a hill beside the lake, right on the edge of town, and his backyard was the most direct and convenient short-cut for kids to get down to Silver Lake. That route was so regular that there was a clear path made both summer and winter. But Thorlief didn't mind the kids cutting through his yard; after all, they weren't doing anything so terribly wrong by that action. Other actions were on the way.

On this cold winter day the kids came flying through his yard once again, swinging their skates over their shoulders and heading for another after-school skating session. (I was one of those kids.)

At the lake shore the dozen or so youngsters sat down either on the bank or on fallen trees and prepared to put on their skates. Most kids had modern shoe-skates but some boys, however, were still using their folks' clamp-on types, the kind that fits badly to the bottom of your boots, the kind that the wearer tries to make a tight-fit by twisting the skate-key so hard that the thumb and forefingers get numb. Even after that effort, the clamp-on skates still seemed to fall off at the slightest pressure.

Eventually all the kids were out on the ice; eventually all got to playing crack-the-whip, with the poor kid at the end getting snapped off and sent hurtling to the middle of the lake. Eventually all got to playing a two-sided game we called prisoners-goal. Eventually all got tired of all of the above, which functions were semi-decent and organized. Civility then stopped as the boys started chasing the girls in what was their junior-high-age version of courting. Not knowing what mating-rights were socially acceptable, the boys demonstrated their affections for the girls by shoving snow down their coat collars. Somehow the girls were supposed to like this curious if cold crude love, but they didn't.

There was a direct correlation between a girl's attractiveness and the cave-man attention paid to her, so that the prettiest girls of all were in semi-danger of their lives from the boys who wanted to demonstrate their carnal interests by first throwing a cross-body-block on them, then washing their faces roughly with snow.

Eventually, thank goodness, all skaters were physically wearying from this Neanderthal behavior and were ready for something else. At this propitious moment the prettiest and most wornout girl of all said; "It's starting to get dark. Let's build a fire."

"Great idea!" exclaimed all the boys. "C'mon, let's gather sticks and boughs and logs and get a real big bonfire going!"

So off we scattered to make our contribution to this planned conflagration. Soon a fire on the ice started out, as little as a mole-hill, then grew a little bigger, then bigger yet as tree limbs and wood from a rotted boat got tossed wholesale onto the roaring blaze.

The fire seemed just right in size; kids could take off their mittens and choppers and warm their red cold hands from five feet away. Some girls suggested, however, that if we boys were any men at all, we'd have a fire that wouldn't just heat the gang there, it would heat the whole county. Whatta challenge!

"Okay, you betcha! Let's make it a REALLY BIG FIRE," said a boy whose name even now, years later, I'd best not mention. "And I know what'll really burn BIG," he added triumphantly.

"What?" said this special girl, who to all the boys was positively lubricious.

"TIRES!"

"Tires?" she replied innocently to her want-to-be young lover. "Do tires burn?"

"Do tires burn?" replied her Lothario with fulsome satire. "Burn? Is Tojo a Nip? Is Hitler a Kraut? Of course they burn! Heck, lemme show you. I saw some old throw-a-way tires next to Thorlief's garage. I'll run up there and get 'em and roll 'em down the hill and you guys throw 'em on the fire."

He did, and we did. One by one Thorlief Egli's precious Goodyears came rolling down the hill, and one by one we tossed them on the raging fire. They burned beautifully, just beautifully. We soon had flames leaping twenty-five feet high into the black sky! Beautiful. The girls were impressed, too.

The tire-fire was eventually burning with such high intensity, and made such a loud noise, that it would have taken a very loud voice indeed to be heard over the din.

But we heard it, all right, heard the voice, heard him, heard the hysterical Thorlief Egli wail so loud that he sounded like a one-man tribe of Banshees screaming down the hill towards that lake and coming at us. Amid his wails came curses—in both English and Norwegian—and intermingled among all the shouting were high-pitched threats promising extreme bodily injury towards the perpetrators of that most foul act of sin.

Skaters flew helter-skelter away from the inferno, away from Thorlief, and out into the blackened night with Thorlief close behind. Only Thorlief's not wearing skates to catch us saved the community from the first manslaughter trial the town might ever have had.

To add injury to insult, poor Thorlief slipped on the ice, fell in a big pile and lay there spread-eagled. He just lay there screaming and swearing, foam oozing gently from this planned-murderer's mouth.

That essentially was the end of it, as far as the kids were concerned. Downtown the next day the men-folk had a big laugh, followed by a statement of sorrow and easy identity with the tire-less, car-less Thorlief. Although it might have been over, it would be another ten years before one school child took the short-cut through Thorlief Egli's backyard again.

Right Question, Wrong Timing

The narrow path running from the house to the barn was hard to walk on even in good weather; in bad weather the rough and bumpy ground made it even more difficult to traverse; and in the wintertime, when slippery ice lay in hidden splotches along the packed snow, the path was absolutely treacherous.

Nevertheless, whatever the condition of the path, the missus made the trip both morning and night, each time lugging two pails of fresh milk back to the kitchen, milk achieved by hand-milking the herd. Uff da. Hard work.

"Ma," as her immigrant husband addressed her as though she had no given name, "Ma milks those critters just right," he said, and added a faint left-handed bit of praise: "She's better than any hired man. Stronger than most, too. Takes strong hands."

She was a strong woman, all right, strong in will as well as hands. The strong will showed up regularly as she kept learning more and more about her new country. She picked up what American farm women do—and what they don't do. They don't do field work, she learned, and left the back-forty hay-rake for good after the neighbor-lady had spied her when the neighbor was in the woods picking blackberries. Embarrassing. Well, embarrassing to get caught. Fee-scum, the shame of it all.

Ma also refused to tend the cattle when they grazed during the day along the township roads and ditches. Grazing cows was kids' work in America, not a chore for wives.

Ma's next American-ways plan was to get out of the milking chores and simply stay in the house, there to cook and wash and do the housework and take care of their three small children. A woman's place was in the home! That's what the women told her at Ladies Aid. Yet the milking remained her job. Home included the barn—and those big-eyed cows. That big Holstein—Emma, by name—along with the five Guernseys— Julia, Edna, Bertha, Hilda and Dora—were her cows, her chores and her chore. If only she could find the right excuse not

After the incident and accident of Ma, Pa would take over 'the ladies' and carry his own blame milk.

to go and milk "the ladies," as Pa called them, every morning and night, every day, every weekend, every month, every year. She and Pa didn't own the cows as much as the cows owned them. She was never free. Oh to be done with that milking!

Given the right reason, she'd quit the milking chores at the flick of a cow's tail. She had said as much many times. The right reason came along unexpectedly in every way.

The chores finished, the pails filled with foaming warm milk, Ma was struggling once again up the rugged path towards the house. It was March. The ice had melted the day before, but froze again during the night, and now at sunrise the blackened ice along the dirty path required tricky footwork, especially when balancing two filled-to-the-brim galvanized pails.

She eased carefully along the path, taking little mincing steps, the kind used when going out on a newly frozen lake during the season's first cold snap. Then Ma found a stretch of easy-going and her steps got longer; but then appeared a five-foot strip of solid ice and her tiny steps became measured in inches. Every trip on that path was an adventure.

For reasons known only to the muses, Pa was watching her labors that morning through the kitchen window, and surprisingly she too glanced up to catch his gaze, far away as it was. She shouldn't have looked up because on that very next step her foot came down on a rut and turned sideways, and in quickly trying to correct that misstep her other foot hit a patch of ice, and before she could holler Holy Hannah, her legs had both flipped up high in the air and down she came, landing flat on her back while the back of her head whacked the frozen path so hard that she saw stars amid the morning sun. She just lay there moaning.

In her pain and agony she saw more than stars when her husband ran quickly out on the back porch and hollered at her crumpled body the question that made her see blood:

"DID YOU SPILL THE MILK?"

And that was the end of chore-time for Ma.

The Migration of the Norwegians to Minnesota

It seems that many centuries ago many Norwegians came to Ireland to escape the bitterness of the Norwegian winters. Ireland was having a famine at the time and food was quite scarce. The Norwegians were eating almost all of the fish caught in the area leaving the Irish with nothing but potatoes. St. Patrick, taking matters into his own hands like most Irishmen do, decided the Norwegians had to go. Secretly he organized I-R-A-J-R-I-O-N (Irish Republican Army to Rid Ireland of Norwegions). Irish members of I-R-A-J-R-I-O-N sabotaged all power plants in hopes that the fish in Norwegian refrigerators would spoil, forcing the Norwegians to a colder climate where the fish would keep. The fish spoiled all right, but the Norwegians, as everyone knows today, thrive on spoiled fish. Forced with a failure, the Irishmen sneaked into the Norwegian fish storage caves in the dead of night and sprinkled the rotten fish with lye, hoping to poison the Norwegian intruders. But as everyone also knows, this is how "lute-fisk" was introduced to the Norwegians and they thrived on this lye-soaked smelly fish. Matters became even worse for the Irishmen when the Norwegians started taking over the Irish potato crop and making lefse. Poor St. Patrick was at his wits end and finally on March 17th he blew his top and told all the Norwegians to go to Hell, and it worked. All the Norwegians left Ireland and moved to Minnesota!

Said the village cynic on a bad March 20: "In Scandinavia it only snowed twice last week—once for three days and once for four days."

SPRING

Misinterpretation Station; Back-Seat Banter

Both men sat in the back seat of the car, a volunteer driver having offered to take them to church. Both men were elderly first generation Norwegian-Americans; both had lived in the same area but only one had lost his Scandinavian accent; both were convivial men who enjoyed a joke and they obviously planned to make cordial conversation together; both felt they now knew the answers—but nobody asked them the questions anymore; and both men were very hard of hearing, and therein lay the problem for their dialog. Their discussion was a kind of non-conversation because of one or two missed or misunderstood words:

★　★　★　★　★

"Ay used to come up here, den, an' buy heffers," said Knute Hokesvig, pointing out the car window at a small herd of cattle off to the left.

"What?"

"HEFFERS!"

"Okay, then; yeah, I liked Herefords too, when it came to beef cattle," replied Arne Lioien. "They raise a lot of 'em still in Nor-Da-Ko-Da."

"Huh?"

"I said they had them in DAKOTA!"

"Aaaa, yeah-shoooooer, ve took da Decorah **Posten**, tew. Gewd newspaper, dat. Azs a kid ay like dat Per and Ole cartoon yokes."

"Yah-yah-yah. I liked Ole and Lena jokes, too. Sometimes. But they sometimes got a little raw. Sometimes, not always. There were some good ones! Hey, did you hear the story about the Green Bay Packers and Ole and Lena?"

"Hvat? Ay miss dat las' part yew say, den."

"OLE AND LENA!"

"Olepheena. Yup, dat iss a funny name for a girl, den. 'Cept ay had a cussin name o' Olepheen. Yew prob'ly coulda knowed her first hussband, Per Haslestad. Poor guy got da vorst case of pyorrhea ay effer seed!"

"Got gonorrhea? For shame! Must have been cattin' around sporting-houses. My uncle had a brother who once picked up a case of clap. Hoot-dee-too! Did he ever suffer from a bad case!"

"Vell, den, my youngest boy Tollef—he lewk middle-age nowdayss—he also suffer from bad case o' Blatz. Musta been ga-reen batch o' beer, an' he da-rink ten bottles! Kids, dey neffer learn to stay way frum bad boose."

"What?"

"BAD BOOSE!"

"Oh, yeah, a caboose. Not a train ever goes by but I have to stare at that last little red car."

"Hvatjasay?"

"I said RED CAR!"

"Diss car don' lewk red to me. Lewks kinda black-ish, but not red-ish. 'Sides, ay neffer like red-ish anyvay."

"Me neither. Give me a good cucumber over a radish anytime. But I got to be careful what I eat on account of my teeth. Heck, when I sink my teeth into a tough steak, they stay there. And that's my favorite part."

"My fav'rit part of da paper iss 'Fifty Yearss Ago Tewday.' 'Cept hven ay lewk, ay gotta hol' da head so high counta da trifocals. Dat git me tired."

"Me too. I get tired just playing checkers. Uff da, then, but there seem to be times when I sit in the rocker just tryin' to get it going."

"Dialin' long-distance vears me out, tew. Hard to keep up da pace."

"Now that you mention pacemakers, did you hear about Skol Skogen? His pacemaker makes the garage door go up everytime he sees a pretty girl go by."

"Yeah-da, den, time shooo-er duss fly. Da only exercise ay git dese dayss iss actin' azs a pallbearer."

By this time they had arrived at their destination. The car slowed down, almost stopped, then turned into the graveled driveway leading to the church. Both men stopped talking and looked at the building, obviously pleased at the sight of a familiar friend.

"Now that you mention pacemakers, did you hear about Skol Skogen? His pacemaker makes the garage door go up everytime he sees a pretty girl go by."

"Vell, den, ve're here, den. Dat trip don' take long in diss new-fangled gas-gussler."

"Yup, this gol-danged fussy pastor sure does talk long. A regular windbag! His sermons always last a half-hour, and he should know that nobody gets saved after twenty minutes. Know what that reminds me of?"

"Ay glad yew ask me. Reminds me uff dat goofy Snoose Skurvik, dat nut. He vonce ask new min'ster: 'Do yew safe fallen vomen?' An' hven he say 'Yah,' Snoose he say, 'Den safe vun for me for Satiddy night!' Hoo-hoo! But y'know? Dat Snoose, **han var pakk** (he was trash).

"What? I missed your last word."

"PAKK."

"Oh, thank-you. And good luck to you, too. As my father always said, **har det bra** (have it good).

"Effreybody alvays tay me ay lewk like my Pa. Vell, time for schurch. Tiss been gewd time to wissit for us."

How do you avoid getting stiff in the joints?
You keep out of those joints!

"My missus passed away ten years ago. But she went fast, and that's the way to go. Flat on your back one minute, then out you go."

"Vell, den, my back goess out more often den ay do."

"Say, I see you forgot your belt to buckle."

"Yah-da, my knees buckle an' my pants von't. Tuff to git old."

"I'd get gold for investment if I were younger, but my pension and social security shecks take care of me. C'mon, ve'd better get going."

"Say, den, tiss time to git goin', issn't it?"

"Yes, and it was nice visiting with you, too."

Diphtheria Days, and Healing Hands

The family stood whispering at the bottom of the stairway, all there except for the sick boy lying on the bed upstairs. The family members then listened intently to the words of a short man with a mustache who was putting instruments into his little black bag:

"He is a very sick young lad," said the doctor, talking in somber tones. "He has...well, I'm very sorry to have to tell you that my first diagnosis was correct." And knowing what disease was meant, the father became ashen-faced while the mother had to reach for a chair to lean on for support. The small boys there listening did not understand what was going on.

I will take care of him, then," said the mother quietly and simply. "I will nurse him back to health again."

"Given the toxic nature of the illness, and the contagiousness of the disease of the patient. . ." and the voice of the medical man trailed off, then came back: "I want you to understand the grave risk that you are taking, madam."

"There is no risk to consider." responded the mother in the same quiet manner. "He is my son. I will make him well again."

The two little boys standing there hearing all this were bewildered. It was all so mysterious and frightening. Upstairs lay their big brother and they knew he was awful sick just by looking at the faces of their parents. Then there were those big words they didn't know like "toxic" and "contagious" and "high mortality rate."

But they also heard the mother say that she would cure the sick boy, and if she said so, then it must be true, because this mother never lied.

The next day the county health officer came and tacked a big sign on the house, right at the top of the front-porch steps: "QUARANTINE! No Admittance. DIPHTHERIA. By the Order of the County Board of Health."

The father moved all the family's essential clothes and bedroom things from upstairs to downstairs where makeshift beds were set up for everyone, but the father never went near the bedroom upstairs with the closed door. Inside that strange room were the sick boy and the mother, and the little boys were not to see their mother again for the next ten days.

The boys had strictest orders from their father never to advance or step up those stairs: "If I catch you doing that, THERE'LL BE WAR!" But the father would put on a gauze mask that made him look so strange, and he would carry trays with towels and sheets and pills and food and quietly take them upstairs, lay the tray on the floor when he got close to the bedroom door and gently push the tray with a broom the rest of the way to the front of the door; then he'd hurriedly leave. When he returned, the tray would be empty.

Neighbor ladies started to come to the house bringing casseroles and jello salads and fresh-baked bread and rolls for the family. The women spoke mainly to the father, but a couple talked to the little boys and told them how strong and brave their mother was.

The boys didn't know quite what to make of that line. Their mother strong and brave? No one ever said that to them before. Gee, as far as they knew, she was just their Mom.

And yet the boys were glad when the women came with food because then they would not have to eat their father's cooking. Father meant well, but he was a terrible cook.

The ladies no doubt meant well in what they said, too, but sometimes words slipped out that scared the boys, like when they overheard Agnes Voie whispering to Thelma Krostuen: "Ay hear hee's not gonna make it, and hee's such a young t'ing to die."

"She had those special, gentle hands that when they touched you on your hot forehead, why you actually felt better immediately. Their Mom had magic hands."

Die? Who's gonna die? He wouldn't die. Their big brother wouldn't die. Their mom would fix him up well again. She said so. And she could do it; she could do anything like that. She had those special, gentle hands that when they touched you on your hot forehead, why you actually felt better immediately. Their Mom had magic hands.

★   ★   ★   ★   ★

There was not much consolation at grade school for the boys, who were suddenly treated like lepers by their former playmates. No one would play with them. "My Pa he sess to stay 'way from you two," exclaimed the fleeing Nels Thompson when the boys tried to get into a game of "Captain-May-I" at recess time.

That's all right, the little boys kept telling themselves, we don't want to play with you guys anyway. But still it hurt. It hurt to be kept out of the gang; it hurt to look up and catch the sneaky glances of former friends who looked away as soon as they saw you were looking at them; it hurt more when kids' whispers included talk about undertakers and funerals. But nobody was going to no funeral! Their Mom would see to that.

Their Mom's presence was there again when they put on their wraps to go home from school. Except for the shoes which came from an uncle in Detroit, every article of clothing they wore—underwear and outerwear—was made by their mother. The boys didn't understand anything about any Depression. And besides, their jackets were warm, their pants fit pretty good, and the hand-knit wool mittens, scarves, and stocking caps kept out the chill of the winds, if not the chilling remarks of insensitive classmates, one who hollered at them as they left the school yard:

"Hey, then, I hear your big brudder ain't gonna pull through. Too bad, too, 'cause he was a good ballplayer. Better than the two of you will ever be together."

The long, dreary, mile-walk home from school each night had become a routine journey of drudgery. With Dad at work, there was no one to go home to. So as usual this day the boys poked along. They kicked away at the bigger stones along the graveled road; they stopped to inspect some gopher holes, threw rocks at the telephone poles, all this as they meandered back to the big brick house at the edge of the village limits.

As they neared their home this tenth day, both boys looked up at the same time to see at a distance their mother standing there on the front porch. And the little boys started running and they ran and ran all the way until they ran into the outstretched arms of their mother.

The same loving arms wrapped themselves around them; the same loving hands touched the back of their necks and pulled them closer together; the same loving voice told them that their big brother was going to be all right, that the fever had broken and that he was breathing well again; the same loving mom told them they would soon all be together and happy again. But then the boys kinda knew that already. After all, their mother had told them so before, and little boys believe their mother.

Addendum: The "little boys," of course, were my brother Robert and myself. Our brother Loren had this dreaded diphtheria, this once terrible scourge of families in the 1930's, but he recovered with no ill effects. It might be added that my mother physically was never a strong woman; indeed, she was somewhat frail. But when it came to devotion to duty, she had the strength of a Samson. As to her hands—ahh, those hands—I shall never forget the comforting feeling of her hands if I live to be 100. My mother, at this writing, is 89, blind, and in a nursing home in Wittenberg, Wisconsin.

(Final post-script. The above column was written and timed to be a kind of Mother's Day present for my mother, and a nurse read it to her when it was published. A month later, when I went to visit her, my mother indicated that she remembered this diptheria-event very vividly; however, she thought she should make it clear that her hands were not really magic and to suggest as much would be untruthful. She explained it this way: "The only magic was a mother's love coming through her hands. It's the magic that every loving mother possesses when she has a sick child.")

Cars and Gals and Dancehalls

"Just how CAN we get there?" pleaded Kari Erickson to her school pal Gudren Moe, who added her part to the drama by wailing the line: "It'll be *thee* dance of the year, I betcha."

"Who's playing?" asked Maren Jorgenson, who just walked in on her friends' conversation.

"Y'mean you haven't heard?" replied the incredulous Gudren. "It's Punky Nockleby and His Concertina Orchestra! He's the best band in the whole county! He can play both old-time AND new-time music!"

Then came her lament: "And we can't get a ride to the Pavilion to hear it." With a glimpse of hope, she asked: "Can you get your dad's car, Maren?"

"Naw, my folks are going to some dumb **bygdelag** (old-home-society) reunion that day and won't be home till midnight, probably all tanked up. How 'bout you, Kari?"

"Never! Pa won't let me go with the car over ten miles from home. 'Sides he says 1941 Cheverolets were made to go to church, not to dancehalls. Pa sure can be a drip sometimes. How 'bout your car, Gudren?"

"Nope. My father says our '42 Ford is on its last legs. He says he wants to buy a new one, now that the war is over, but he

---

" 'Sides he says 1941 Cheverolets were made to go to church, not to dancehalls. Pa sure can be a drip sometimes."

---

says the prices are too blame high and he's gonna wait until car prices drop. My dad's so tight that he squeaks."

"Whad'll we DO?" wailed Kari once again. "Punky's band's really keen, y'know? He turns me into a screamy-meemy, y'know?"

"I know. And I know how we can get to the Bear Lake Ballroom, too," said the thoughtful Maren. "Just use the same way and the same guy we use when we want a ride anywhere."

"BARNIE BRUBAKKEN!" said Kari and Gudren together, with Kari then wrinkling up her nose and adding: "He's such a jerk. And he drives like Barney Oldfield. And he talks like he just got off the boat from the old country. And he smells so awful of barn! Pewey!"

"So he stinks of the stable? Who cares? We'll open the window; we'll smoke our Marvels and fumigate the car," replied the practical Maren. "Lest we ever forget, girls, Barnie owns his own car! There's NOTHING more important than that."

"Ain't that sumpin', though," sighed Kari, "the only boy in the whole high school with wheels of his own, and it has to be that icky Barnie Brubakken. Well," she added, now getting down to the nitty-gritty, "whose turn is it to con him into a ride this time?"

"Not me."

"Me neither."

"Why not? You brought him up, and it's your turn, Maren. And you know there's nothing to it. The same plan always works: you sidle up to Barnie, bat your eyelashes, wiggle your hips, swirl your skirt, and when he's still pushin' his eyeballs back in place, ask him for a ride to this or that party or this or that ball game, and then Barnie gets red in the face from excitement, thinking he's finally got a date with a real girl."

"Yeah," added Maren, picking up the formula, and ready to volunteer to carry it through. "I know what to do. Two minutes after he croaks out that big Norsk 'Yah!' of his, I go back and tell him that I've already promised a friend that she could go along, and then of course my friend needs to bring her friend, and before he knows it, the car is all filled with girls—and Barnie hauls 'em all." And then they all laughed and prided themselves at how clever they were. Big dumb smelly Barnie. Putty in their hands.

Barnie Brubakken stood by the school water bubbler, all alone, as usual. A gangly, horse-faced lad who stood out from the crowd because he seemed at least one generation behind his age group.

While other boys wore pink, shell-rimmed glasses that were so popular after the second world war, Barnie had round wire-rims; while others had close-cropped crew cuts, Barnie wore his hair long, parted in the middle, and slicked down tight with Brilliantine goop; while other guys dressed with a certain planned sloppiness in their corduroy pants and too-large-sweatshirts, Barnie came along with his shiny gabardine slacks and cheap white dress shirts with their starched collars.

(And under all of this dated, sartorial mess Barnie wore long-underwear, the one piece variety with the trap-door in the back.)

Barnie always smelled of barn, despite even the principal's urging him to change his clothes—and wash—after chores before coming to school. All to no avail. His real name was Bjarne, but he was always called Barnie, short for Barnsmell.

Maybe Barnie didn't have any friends—but he sure had a car! He drove a 1938 Terraplane, a unique vehicle in itself, but the way Barnie drove it, the car was renamed The Terrible Plane. Barnie-the-Terror in his Terrible Plane.

   Barnie Barnsmell might observe, "The only lie that I can
tolerate is a beautiful blonde telling me that I get better looking every day!"

"Hi-ya, Bjarne," said the sweet voice of Maren as she approached the water cooler, pretending she needed a drink. "Sure nice day, huh?" she added in tones of honey dripping from her lips. She then tossed her chest out and her head back, and she pretended to be fixing her upswept hair-do, a style which she thought made her look like actress Yvonne DeCarlo.

"Yew talkin' ta me?"

"Sure am, Bjarne. Gee, but you're tall! And hey, I heard you got a new colt born out at your place."

"Yew betcha! A strawberry roan. A real humdinger!" Barnie was warming up to the situation—and being set up at the same time.

"Say Bjarne, 'y'know 'bout that dance comin' up Saturday night at the Pavilion? Well, how'ja like to take me? Huh? How 'bout it? Huh?"

Barnie looked suddenly very serious. "Maren, y'know our min'ster he sess Sunday dat dancin' is sinful, and dancehalls iss evil places, and kids who go to dem ballroomss is goin' ta hell! An' ay sure not vant to go to dat placce. Dat's vorse den school!"

"Y'mean, y'mean you won't take us? I mean me," shrieked the shaken Maren.

"Dass vright," said Barnie, now puttin' on his pious face. "Dey da-rink boose and sin in dose awful places. An' asz my mudder sess it: 'Boosers iss loosers, and sinnerss iss neffer vinnerss.'"

"Barnie?"

"Yeah?"

"Cram it."

Basketball in "The Olden Days"

March is Madness Month.

The term madness can be applied for several reasons, including the fact that March is high school basketball tournament time.

For a few weeks there is a kind of madness affecting towns and teams, parents and principals, cheerleaders and chambers of commerce. There is this brief moment each year for many citizens when basketball rates just ahead of the Second Coming in importance.

March Madness has gone on for half a century and will likely go on another fifty years and more. Not much has changed, say some; it's always been this way, say others.

Not so. Not true. Certain things about basketball have changed immensely, notably the facilities used, the tempo of the game (there used to be a centerjump after every basket made); even the school yells have been altered.

Such changes can be easily noted by observing basketball in the many lutefisk ghettoes around the midwest where the game was and is still played with near-hysterical enthusiasm.

At one time school basketball had a definite ethnic flavor, a flavor since altered by the melting-pot concept and that **ongoing** process called Americanization.

Before all this amalgamation, however, consider the following high school cheer from Chicago's Lane Technical high school in the early 1930's:

JA JA JA, HVAD SKAL DU HA?
(Yes yes yes, what do you want?)
TI CENTER LUTEFISK, JA JA JA.
(Tens cents of lutefisk)

Or a crowd-rousing cheer from Portland, North Dakota, in the mid 1940s:

TA DEM PAA NAKKEN
(Take them by the neck)
SLAA DEM PA BAKKEN
(Slam them on the ground)
JA, JA, DET GAAR BRA
(Yes, yes, it goes well)
PORTLAND HIGH SCHOOL
RAH RAH RAH.

Or a cheer from Scandinavia, Wisconsin, in the late 40s:
LUTEFISK OG LEFSE
(Lutefisk and lefse)

GAMEL OST OG PRIM
(old cheese and special)
SCANDINAVIA HIGH SCHOOL
BASKETBALL TEAM.

And a slight variation of the same from Clermont, Iowa, in the mid 1950's:
LUTEFISK OG LEFSE
TAKK SKAL DU HA
(Thanks you shall have)
CLERMONT HIGH SCHOOL
RAH RAH RAH.

As for facilities, well, today's squad members who perform in these well-lighted palatial complexes, with see-through glass backboards and seating in the bleachers for hundreds of fans, will likely never know the pioneering that went before them.

Nowadays it seems peculiar—bordering on the awesome —what town structures could be and were used as basketball courts:

The Community Hall—built for every purpose except basketball—became a court by merely painting some lines and putting up two baskets mounted on wooden backboards. Never mind that the heat-register was in the middle of the center jump circle; never mind that a long shot required shooting over the beams; never mind that the three painted circles all overlapped each other. After all, a short court made each trip up and down that much shorter and the game that much faster, albeit congested.

The local Armory became another make-shift arrangement that would serve as a court and save Scandinavian taxpapers *mange penger* (much money). Never mind that the floor buckled in the middle; that out-of-bounds meant a player had touched one of the spectators who sat on the one and only row of plank benches that encircled the floor. After all, this seating arrangement allowed fans literally to get into the "baska-ball games."

The trade-show Pavilion at the local fair grounds was another convenient court for The Game to go on. Never mind that the

Did you hear about the basketball game between the Norwegians and the Swedes? The Swedes got mad and went home, and after 45 minutes the Norwegians won the game when they made a basket!

ceiling was only four feet higher than the basket; that one end was brilliantly lighted while the other end was almost dark; never mind that there were no shower or toilet facilities (where the latrine for the team was an empty three-pound can of Hills Bros. coffee). After all, if a better facility was required, there was that two-holer available just 50 feet behind the Pavilion.

The prize for a used or misused building serving as a basketball court should go to this town (best not named) where the playing floor was L-shaped. Never mind that players could look up after snagging a rebound and not see the basket at the other end; never mind that there was a need for a sharp right-hand turn on a fast break; and never mind that when one drove in for a lay-up—and someone had left the outside door open—the player landed outside in a snowbank. After all, seldom can open doors contribute so much action to an otherwise dull game.

Some of these pioneering problems were compensated for by blond, blue-eyed cheerleaders whose last names all ended in SON; they would bound out to the center of the floor with an audience-response yell that will never be heard again on an American high school playing floor:

Skal vi ha vic-try?
JA JA JA
Skulle vi gaa hjem utafor?
NEI NEI NEI.
De er saa bra, de er saa godt
Det er saa fint at de var bødt!
AKKURAT AKKURAT AKKURAT!
(Shall we have victory?
(Yes, yes, yes
(Should we go home without it?
(No no no.
They are so nice, they are so good
(It is so fine that they were born.
(Exactly, exactly, exactly!)

It was the best of times, it was the worst of times. . . JA, JA, JA.

Explaining the difference between "Uff Da" and "Fee Da."
"Uff Da" is what you say when you drop the garbage. "Fee
Da" is what you say when you step in it!

The School Band Blues

Strong, big-boned farmwives squeezed and squirmed themselves into their children's grade-school desks. Corseted bodies tested the product as the ladies took extra deep breaths before forcing torsoes between the wooden desk-edges and the slat-backed seats that didn't budge an inch.

Anna Amundson, a lady of considerable girth, eyed her son's desk in front of her, took mental measurements, then walked away and picked up a solid but tiny fifth-grader's reading-chair, and she hunkered down on top of that. (The scene was akin to Orson Welles today sitting on a milk stool.)

Some fathers, too, had come grudgingly to the band concert, with one complaining to the ticket seller (admission was ten cents): "Da band shewd pay da peeple yust fer showin' up, den."

Even the proper Mrs. Stamstad, the minister's wife, was there, although she had no child performing, but her attendance was the proper thing to do. Mrs. Stamstad was very proper and by her manner and manners, she bestowed on the community the example of how proper people should act properly. Or, as the men on the bench in front of the hardware store phrased it, "Dat Missuss Stamstad, she vouldn't say crap, den, iff she had a mout'ful."

There were few if any frills attached to grammar school extra curricular activities during the late Depression and early War years. Thus it was remarkable that our tiny grade school had a band, of sorts, which put on a concert, of sorts, once a year.

The band was both tiny and cheap. It was composed of one coronet, one trumpet, two trombones, one clarinet, one saxophone, a tuba, a snare drum, and a bass drum, the latter three instruments on loan from the Union Free high school. The local RFD mailman, who played in a World War I Army band, donated his time and directed the alleged musicians.

Within the group were two superb players, one a red-haired, freckled-faced coronet player whose bashed-in horn had been purchased for twelve dollars from one of the town drunks. The other good musician was a trombone player whose almost new Conn horn came as a result of his father's short-lived success as a silver-fox farmer. (Both young boys would later distinguish themselves in adulthood as outstanding band directors.)

The quality of the rest of the band, however, ranged from fair to lugubrious. Among the very worst was the trumpet player, Torger "Snag" Forde (his nickname of Snag came because of his habit for having long boogers snagged to his nose). Now Snag Forde couldn't read words in a book, let alone music on a score. He couldn't follow a skunk with a nosebleed down a snowcovered back-alley. Yet he had the only new horn, the benefit of a solicitous father who owned one of the town's two general stores.

(The father's tightness in running his store was reflected in his breaking cookies in half when weighing them on a scale; people got the exact measure, but no more!)

In this Scandinavian ensemble was only one girl, a fair saxophone player named Ingeborg Swenson. She was a tiny girl whose physical growth towards maturity was obvious in one area only, her chest; there she was wondrously over-compensated for by nature, and Snag Forde constantly eyed the growth pattern.

(Ingeborg's father was the local Lutheran Brotherhood agent who believed that each policy he sold was an act of near-divine mercy on his part. He has to be one of the rare insurance peddlers who expects a new policy recipient to first offer a handshake and then concomitant thanks to the agent for the lucky fortune of being saved by Lutheran Brotherhood.)

The tuba player was good, but he had no wind. His shortness of breath was caused by his smoking too many Wings cigarettes, the weeds purloined from either his father's jacket pocket or Snag's father's store.

The bass drum player was good in that he could keep a steady beat, and that was mandatory as the snare drummer's rhythmic patterns were so erratic that he could disguise the beat in any melody to the point where the audience—and the poor director—did not know if the tune was a polka or a cha-cha-cha.

To compound the problem, the snare drummer wanted to be like his hero, Gene Krupa, and use the drum as a solo instrument. Thus he pounded the poor drum-hide with a ferocity bordering on the demonic.

Torben Gausdal, Junior, held a clarinet; he never played it, he just held it. He got the instrument because it showed up as a surprise at the bottom of a cardboard box bought by Torben, Senior, at a sheriff's auction.

The father-and-son Gausdals had much in common. Both exhibited definite simian characteristics, and both had the **couth** of orangutans. (Once the exasperated director asked the younger Gausdal what he wanted to be, and his answer: "A billy goat." Naturally the father was thrilled, as any father whose son aspired to follow in his steps.)

(If the reader is counting, the one remaining band member is the second trombone player, myself. My musical gifts, I was gently informed then, perhaps lay in the field of vocal music.)

The special concert—and oh! but it was a special—began with a march called "Our Director," a number that was lively and likeable and best of all, playable. It was a piece that made the mothers beam with pride and the fathers forget briefly about the Joe Louis—Buddy Baer fight a week away.

Then came a waltz. At least it started out and ended as a waltz, although somewhere in the middle the snare drummer tried to turn it into a fox trot.

The third number, a long overture, should never have been attempted. The slowness and interminable length of the first section put Torben Gausdal, Senior, to sleep, and not even his subsequent snoring was that bad, but it was in this conked-out state that Torb lifted one over-alled cheek and passed gas with a thunderous blast.

At that point the concert began to unravel. Almost all in the audience pretended that they never heard a thing, and though the thunderclap could maybe be overlooked, the resulting odor could not. In this hot, crowded room that held perhaps thirty people, it was impossible to pretend that nothing gross had happened, especially when it was noticed that Mrs. Stamstad's manner suggested her fainting—from embarrassment.

Then Torben, Junior, matching the social proprieties of his still-snoozing father, put down his clarinet to whisper loudly enough for all in the room to hear: "Who cut the cheese?"

Now the director may not have been a musical nor socio-logical genius, but he had common sense, and he knew when to close off a performance forthwith. Thus three baton beats later the director brought down both his arms with finality in a manner that said with lying conviction: this is the end of this piece! And with that he turned around and announced a brief (and blessed) intermission. For such quick thinking, his audience would forever remain eternally grateful.

It's amazing how most concerts attended are soon forgotten. It takes something special for one to recall a specific perform-ance, and the above-mentioned concert shall never be forgot-ten, alas.

Troubled Times; Tampering With 'Theology'

When immigrants came to America from Norway, among the first of their institutions established was the church. In this way they laid the foundations not only for the eventual large and powerful bodies of Lutheran churches among Scandinavians, but also for the strife and dissension that marked the development.

Noted Norwegian-American author Einar Haugen wrote: "Between the low-church element, which eventu-ally organized itself into the so-called Hauge's Synod, and the high-church followers of the Norwegian Synod, there sprang into being in 1890 a 'middle church' Synod known as the United Norwegian Lutheran Church in America. One more generation led to the dropping of the name 'Norwegian' (1946), and within the next generation the church itself merged into a new American Lutheran Church (1960)." (The Norwegians in America, pp.23-24)

Although there were many issues to divide congregation, one hot problem were changes made in the church-services, these changes reflected in new "hymnals," each with its special color.

For almost half a century, the standard books used in churches were a blue **Concordia** and a black **Lutheran Hymnary.** These books were "gospel"; these books were "right"; these books were "proper," and maybe the only way to Norwegian salvation.

And then along came this merger of Synods, and with that change came a new order of service, along with new hymns—and it was all in one book, and its cover was **RED!**

Torben Borgen, a middle-aged bachelor-farmer, had been absent from Farmington Lutheran Church for over a year, a long recess caused by a combination of congenital illness and congenital stubbornness. Torb was not about to go back to a church where he had heard about the terrible change: his very own congregation had adopted a new hymnbook!

Awful as this might be, curiosity got the better of him, and off he went to a Sunday morning service at 11 a.m., the holiest hour of the week. The result was devastating for poor Torben.

The next morning, right after hurrying through chores, Torben Borgen jumped into his '53 pickup and headed for his neighbor Sigurd Sovde. On the way he tried to dream up an acceptable excuse for the visit, a pretense that would lead to a discussion of the heresy at yesterday's debacle:

"Hei du, Sig, det er kaldt idag" (Hi, Sig, It's cold today). "Yah."

" 'Cept it should varm up by coffee-time."

"Yeah-sure." Sigurd was getting impatient. "You want sumpin', Torb?"

"Sigurd," said Torb with a deep sigh, "vuss yew in schurch?"

"Yah-yah-yah. I wuss there in our regular pew, den."

"Ay vuss in schurch, tew."

"Don't worry, Torb. Everyone saw you. Nobody misses nothin' in that church."

And then Torben exploded: "THUNDERATION! You changed books!"

"Yeah-da, then. We had 'em for 'bout two months now, then."

"Dey're RED!"

"Yeah, so they're red. So what?"

"Dey're COMMUNIST!"

"Ah, shucks, Torb. That's dumb, and you know it."

"Vell, tell me hvat vuss da matter vit da **black** vun?"

"Nuthin', then, I guess. 'Cept the church leaders figured it wuss time for a different service-book, I guess. Both me and the missus like the old black one better, too. And ve sure liked the hymns better from the old blue Concordia."

"Da CON-COR-JA? Now dat had fine moo-sic! Now dey gone an' sca-rewed up effreyting. Tiss da vork of da devil! Dere's songs in dat red monster ay neffer seed before—and dey left out ALL da gewd ol' hymns!"

"Now take 'er easy, Torb, you're gettin' red in the face."

"Fie-da, scum! Can yew blame me? Da 'hole schurch iss changed! Da prest (minister) used to giff da mornin' prayer after da sermon; now it's before! Azz to his chantin' songs, vell, ay t'ought he vuss makin' up new tunes as he vent along. Ay tink dey should take dose new red books and ship 'em to Roosia."

"Well, Torb, all I know is that we sing all them verses of every hymn. If there were forty verses to a hymn, Lutherans would sing every last one of them." Then Sigurd remembered something, and dropped another bombshell: "By the way, Torb, seein' I'm on the board of deacons, I thought you might be interested to know that we've called another preacher."

"You did? Ve are? Vell, ay hope dat diss new guy iss dry behind da earss."

"Well, er...ah, he's kind of different, then. He wears a full beard."

"Aaa, Herre Gud!" (Holy God!)

And he drives a red Olds convertible."

"Hoot ma toot!"

"An' he even told us in his interview that he likes to drink beer now and then!"

"Aa, den store verden! All diss is a shoo-er sign from da Lord dat da end of da vorld iss near."

"Well, I gotta go, Torb. Got work to do. See you in church next Sunday."

"Me? Neffer! Red hymnals and now red pastors! Da Loo-tern schurch iss da las' place you vill find me! Da ta-rew teachin's uff da Lord iss been cor-rupted. Who knows? Next ting dey'll haff iss vomen in da pulpits! Ay tink ay'll yust drop out an yoin da Holy-Rollerss."

It's A Wise Father Who Knows His. . .Neighbors' Children

At the turn of the century in rural America, time was when each new-born infant was welcomed to the farm family as another needed farm hand.

The baby might well be an extra mouth to feed, but he or she was also a potential provider and contributor to the farm economy in the not-too-distant future. Kids went to work early on farms.

This combination of economics, food and fertility led to some very large families, parents whose many offspring sometimes came close to the label of brood. It was not uncommon for a farmer and his wife to produce a dozen or more children, and these large numbers all living under one roof led to some amusing moments of consternation, as once experienced by my mother.

My mother was born in 1895, but as the child of a farmer-turned-Lutheran-minister, there were **only** eight brothers and sisters living in the parsonage at Glenwood township, Decorah, Iowa.

When she was ten years old, she visited a friend at a

". . . she went into the dining room and was seated among the other nineteen children around this huge dining-room table."

neighboring farm where there were nineteen children in the family.

Invited to stay this one night for supper, she went into the dining room and was seated among the other nineteen around this huge dining-room table.

All of the children sat quietly, learning early—and sometimes painfully—from their parents that nobody but nobody either talked or moved one finger towards the food until after the father asked the blessing for all, followed by the mother's high-sign to the group in Norwegian: "Vaer saa gud." (EAT!)

Thus as the twenty heads sat unmoving, in strode the Papa who walked briskly to his place at the head of the table. As was his custom before the prayer, he looked around sternly at each member of his brood, a procedure that took a little while.

It was during his routine once-around-the table gazing that he spied my mother sitting among the flock, which sight caused him to stop, wrinkle his nose, and scratch his head. Then he turned to his wife beside him and asked with a puzzled voice: "Is that one of ours?"

Baseball and Box-Socials; Strange Mixes

Loren Bjorken was having trouble getting his friend Arvid Mork to budge. Stubborn Norwegian, that Arvid, even when Arvid agreed that it was for a good cause, baseball, their favorite sport.

The issue was Arvid's attendance once again at the spring box-social, an event held annually to help raise money for the town baseball team to buy equipment for the forthcoming season of Sunday afternoon baseball, *The* major summer entertainment for most of the community and especially for these two men who were first-row-behind-the-chicken-wire-fence supporters.

Each armed for every contest with a handy-six of Pabst Blue Ribbon beer ("Basic Blue" they called it), each fat and fifty, each balding and bulging, the two bachelors never missed a game at home or away, even when it meant being late for chores. The cows could wait at the barn gate until the ninth inning was over, all for the glory of the Scandinavia Vikings, the town team.

They were Vikings backers all the way—except Arvid was now having doubts about the upcoming box-social. The event itself was all right; in fact it was lots of fun! There was spirited bidding for the nicely wrapped boxes, good-natured kidding back and forth among the bidders, and the lively auctioneer needling the penny-pinchers combined to make the box-social a festive occasion.

Then too there was even a touch of mystery and suspense. After all, each lunch-box sold had the element of surprise: Whose box was it? The winning bidder for each lunch-box got to share that lunch with the lady who prepared the box in the first place, but the preparer's name was a sworn secret, and so the bidders were never sure who their partner would be until after the auctioneer declared the box SOLD! Only then did he announce the lady's name, at which point the audience would react, sometimes with shouts and cheers and applause, but sometimes just silence and sometimes semi-silent snickers.

And there-in lay the problem for Arvid because the past two years he had ended up unhappily in the corner trying to eat lousy tuna sandwiches with Gladyce Lokensgaard, and goofy Gladyce was something else again, something to be avoided. Said Arvid to Loren, regarding his unwanted box-social partner of the past two auctions:

"Shee's a goof!"

"Yah, she iss a li'l looney," agreed Loren.

"She dyess her hair BLUE!"

"Yah, it duss come out dat color—and sometimes it's purple."

"An' her false-tee't vobble."

"Yah-da, den. Shees a li'l short on da Polident."

"An' she jabbers a mile-a-minute, an' sess nut'in."

"Yah. Ay t'ink shee's feeble-minded, but not much. Not tew bad considerin' dat sca-rewball hussban' she got stuck vit. Compared to dat dinggle-berry, Gladyce iss a sixty-four-dollar-qvestion vinner!"

"Vell ay t'ink shees plain nuts. So vill yew tell me vy ay gotta git stuck vit **Dat** voman effrey blame year?"

"Beats me. Ay gas yew mus' yust be lucky den. Hoo hoo hoo."

Despite the smart alect remark and laughter, Loren did persuade Arvid to try the box-social just once more, arguing the irrefutable logic that lightning could not strike him three years in a row. Gladyce Lokensgaard just had to be won by somebody else this year.

"Iss yew shoo-er, den?" asked the doubting Arvid.

"Yahhhhhhhh. Poss-i-tiff," replied the confident Loren. "An' dat night ay'll g'ff yew my secret adwice!"

The Community Hall was buzzing with excitement as Loren and Arvid sidled in. Up on the stage stood the auctioneer—the local lumberyard dealer—and at his feet lay a mound of beautifully wrapped and decorated boxes—usually old shoe boxes—each filled with good things to eat, each waiting for the right bidder.

While the crowd grew a bit impatient waiting for the bidding to start, in staggered Knute Hokesvig, chanting his usual cheer:

"LUTEFISK AND LEFSE, RØMEGRØT AND SNOOSE, SCANDINAVIA VIKINGS LOOSE AS A GOOSE!"

"Dat Knute, yew kin alvays depend on him to show up vit a shine on," muttered a disgusted Loren.

"Yah, hees half-stewed all day and full-stewed all night," added Arvid. "How dat soak managed to buy hiss new '47 Mercury iss more den mos' people can figure out, den. Spiffy car, dat Merc."

"Bah. A Mercury iss nuttin' more den a Ford vit lock-vashers," replied Loren, unimpressed.

Then the auctioneer banged his cane on the cement stage, tipped his corny cowboy hat back on his head, and the auction was ready. At this point Loren leaned over to Arvid and whispered:

"Vanna know da secret on hven an' hvat to buy? Tiss eassy. Buy dat wery first box dat goess up for sale. Tiss sheaper and safer den vaiting till da end, da vay yew dun it. Here, den, lemme show yew," and he stood up tall as the auctioneer said:

"Now who will start out the bid for the first lunch of the evening, folks? Who'll give me three dollars for this bee-oooo-tiful package I got right here in my hand?"

"Ay'll giff yew fifty cents," hollered Loren.

"Only a half a buck?" replied the auctioneer, appearing to be stunned by the offer. "That's mighty small potatoes for something as nice as this," and he held up the box higher for all to see.

"A buck!" came a voice from across the hall, belonging to Bendic Bjorken, Loren's unkissing-cousin, with whom he was still at odds over a hay-fork which he borrowed and never brought back to Loren.

"A dollar and a half!" replied Loren, who didn't like the competition.

"Two big ones!" came the response from Bendic, obviously enjoying the contest, and knowing full well what his cheapskate cousin was up to.

Then entered a new voice: LUTEFISK AND LEFSE, RØMEGRØT AND SNOOSE. . ."

"Shut up! Knute, yew dumb-cluck!" said the auctioneer. "Either get in the bidding or keep quiet."

By now Loren was mad. "Ten bucks!" yelled Loren, and the crowd oohed and applauded. "Howja like dem berries, Bendic?" he hollered at his cousin, ready to take him on in this fight-to-the finish.

"*Det kostet mange penger* (That costs much money,)" answered the beaten Bendic, now willing to concede, but also knowing well that likely not one box the rest of the night would go that high.

"SOLD!" cried the auctioneer, and he brought his cane down firmly. "Sold to Loren Bjorken, for a darn good price, too. And now the preparer of that fine box," he said, his voice trailing off as he searched for the name. "Yessireesir, Loren will share his ten-dollar lunch with none other than. . .lemme see, now here it is, here's the name. Yup. it's Gladyce Lokensgaard."

And the crowd went wild! They cheered and laughed and cheered some more. Arvid just beamed and beamed and said not a word to the crestfallen Loren who was trying so hard to pretend publicly that he was pleased with himself.

"LUTEFISK AND LEFSE, RØMEGRØT AND SNOOSE!" croaked Knute Hokesvig.

"Shut-UP! Or you'll git a poke in the snoot, Knute," threatened the testy Loren. At this point Arvid leaned over and whispered to his friend: "Enjoy da tuna. An' t'anks for yur gewd ad-wice."

A Wag's Tour Norway

12 days — 4 nights
(June Once to June 31) $49.98 per couple

1st Day   Leave Minneapolis airport somewhere between noon and midnight, traveling on Norsk single-engine Dumbo Jet

2nd Day   In Air

3rd Day   In Air

4th Day   In Air

5th Day   Arrive in Oslo-area farmer's field at 9:03½ a.m. or p.m. and on to Oslo Hilton Hotel Basement Annex for box lunch: a cold lutefisk sandwich served in a box. Rest of day spent recovering from lunch.

6th Day   A complete city tour of Oslo, 8:30 - 8:40 a.m. Then free-time for shoplifting, followed at noon by a faboulous 7-course noon lunch (a torsk sandwich and a six-pack)

7th Day   We tour the countryside in the comfort of a rebuilt Norwegian Army Tank

8th Day   Back in Oslo for a tour of the University of Norway (both buildings). Everyone will get to see the book in the Health Science Library

9th Day   Board your thundering Jet to U.S. of A. Only
           three quick stops on the journey, two for fuel and
           one for directions

10th Day   In Air

11th Day   In Air

12th Day   Arrive at American Airport precisely between 6
           a.m. and midnight, depending on weather condi-
           tions and fuel leakage.

DON'T DELAY— Reservations must be received no later
              than departure time. P.S. For safety
              measures, most passengers will be given
              a parachute. Those not receiving one can
              expect to share one with their neighbor.

                         Shot Gunderson
                         Tour Guide*

*To readers appalled by any reference to "Ethnic Dumbness" Jokes comes an
apology: No offense intended.*

Red Hot Runner
Seeks Cold

Butter Blekestad was a cocky kid. He was glib and flip; he
was brassy and sassy, too much so. We knew that some day
soon he'd go too far with his big mouth and get it. He got it.

Butter's real name was David, but his dad was the town
butter-maker at the local creamery and so the son was nick-
named Butter Blekestad, that smart-aleck, fat kid who lived on
the mill-pond.

The ambition of every young boy in town was to become a
star baseball player, and even if one couldn't exactly star, one
could at least be on the squad, a designation that allowed the
boy to receive a baseball uniform, of sorts.

With the high school so small in numbers, it was not difficult
to be picked for the squad. Simply turning out for the sport was

usually enough evidence of interest; athletic abilities, alas, were secondary.

Fat, fourteen and a freshman, Butter had more brass than brains. Out on the baseball diamond he was all-talk-and-no-do. He couldn't run, hit, or field. On the squad of a baker's dozen, Butter was number fifteen. All he could do was talk, and alibi for his mistakes—and make life miserable for anyone else who might miscue.

So it was during a routine after-school practice that all the outfielders were shagging fly balls off the fungo-bat of Aksel Aspebakken, a young man out of high school who came around regularly to help out the one and only coach. Aksel played on the summer town-team, often pitching when his arm was all right.

With the outfielders taking turns, Aksel would whop one arching-flyball after another, and this one time the regular varsity center field, Karl Olson, drifted over to make the catch—and he dropped the ball. But no problem, no big deal, nobody or nothing hurt; after all, it was only an after-school practice.

But Butter Blekestad thought it was a big deal, and he started razzing Karl: "What's wrong, club-foot? Too much goose-grease in the mitt, huh? Need a bigger glove maybe?"

Karl, a long, string-bean farm boy, did not even reply to the taunts. He just looked at the yipping Butter and smiled, but Karl had malice in his eyes. That little dink Butter has got to be dealth with accordingly, said those blue eyes. Still Karl said nothing although Butter kept on ragging him.

The practice for the day ended and all the boys hightailed it for the school shower-room, but on the way Karl stopped, went over to Aksel's pickup, talked quietly with him for a minute, and soon Aksel produced from the glove compartment a jar of "Red Hot," an ointment that pitchers put on their arms when they get sore.

Red Hot spread on the arm and rubbed made the arm warm, even hot. The more rubbing there was, the hotter the skin became. The plot was thickening.

Karl took the jar, stuffed it in his pocket and headed for the shower room. While all the guys—including Butter—were in getting soaked, Karl found Butter's clothes and spread a very ample supply of Red Hot in Butter's shorts.

Afterwards, as Karl was going into the shower, Butter was coming out with his mouth running: "Hi there, you error-filled mistake. You're late. You been out looking for that hole in your glove?"

While all the guys—including Butter—were in getting soaked, Karl found Butter's clothes and spread a very ample supply of Red Hot in Butter's shorts.

Karl gave him a big smile, still said nothing as Butter jerked on his clothes quickly and readied to leave, but not without a parting shot: "Hey then, loser, it's you they should call 'Butter,' short for 'Butterfingers.' Uff da. Well, see you in the pain-factory again tomorrow, Butterfingers. I gotta hurry home now and catch Amos 'n Andy."

Little did he know the speed with which he would hurry home.

Butter started meandering down the school driveway, and by the time he hit the sidewalk towards town, he seemed to sense that something was wrong. Not realizing what had happened, he began rubbing his rear which of course made it all the worse. His pants seemed to be on fire!

Butter's pace picked up considerably, going from a walk to a quick step to a fast jog. The faster he moved, the hotter he got, and the jog turned into a full run. The faster he ran, the more heat was produced, but the equation he did not put together. All he knew was that his hind end was burning up!

Butter also knew that he had to get home as soon as possible and he began flying pell-mell down the sidewalk, running absolutely wide open for half a mile. Although out of breath and gasping for air, he never let up. (The sight of this little fat kid pounding lickety-split down the pavement was a view few neighbors would forget.)

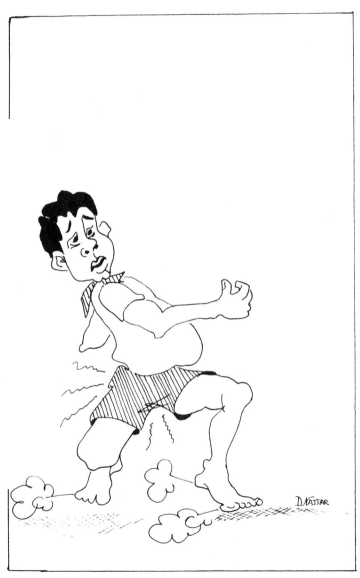

"The sight of this little fat kid pounding lickety-split down the pavement was a view few neighbors would forget."

By the time Butter hit the driveway to his house, he never slowed down. He never slowed down when he got to the house, either; he ran right past that and jumped straight into the mill-pond behind the home. And there he sat, not budging.

His mother, who witnessed the scene, ran out from the kitchen and into the back yard and immediately questioned her son's sanity: "Er du galen?" (Are you crazy?) Butter just sat there in the cool water, not saying a word.

★ ★ ★ ★ ★

Addendum: Somewhere today there are two men, now likely long of tooth and with jowls sagging. But also very likely the two can still conjure up this one event in their lives, and one can close the eyes and picture Karl and Aksel still smiling. Revenge is sweeter when hotter. As for Butter, he turned out fine. At this writing he is a successful superintendent of schools in a large Minnesota city.

Did You Hear the One About the Norwegian. . .

What is delightful to some Scandinavian-Americans is an affront to others; what tickles the funny-bone for many people makes the blood boil for another group; what a few find absolutely hilarious is what a few others find absolutely reprehensible. The issue is ethnic-jokes.

Two middle-aged friends—and they were good friends, which is why they could even discuss the issue somewhat rationally—were in the middle of this topic, complete with stories, complete with alleged-joke responses, complete with sermonizing on both sides.

★ ★ ★ ★ ★

"This Norwegian walked into a store. He had a parrot on his shoulder, and the clerk look up and asked: 'Where'd you get that goofy-looking thing?' And the parrot replied: 'In Norway, they've got a million of them over there.' Har har har!"

"I don't like it."

"Huh? Thought it was pretty good, myself. Heard it from Oscar Bredesen. He had another one, too; how 'bout this one: 'The U.S. State Department just announced that the U.S. is selling Norway 137 septic tanks. Yup, and as soon as they learn how to drive 'em, they're gonna invade Sweden! Hoo hoo! Heard that one once before from Charlie Evanson, but forgot it. He's full of 'em."

"He's full of 'it.' And he should be ashamed of himself. So called ethnic jokes which have as their only point the stupidity of a nationality are insulting, if not dangerous. As a Norwegian-American, I find them offensive."

"As another Norwegian-American, I love 'em. And I don't find them offensive. Neither does Sons of Norway President Charlie Evanson, and he's a full-blooded Norskie, too; and he's always telling Norwegian-stories. Explain that if it's so bad."

"I can't explain it, except to suggest that only vacuous minds tell 'dumb-ethnic' stories. Consider also that all these jokes are interchangeable as to the group being demeaned. It could be **any** group, any nationality."

"That's likely the reason people tell Norskie-stories now. But first of all, you should agree that almost always there is no offense intended by the story tellers; secondly, by **not** singling out nationalities where there are current political and social strife—as in present-day Poland or Ireland—it seems like almost a compliment to choose a Scandinavian country where there are both stability and prosperity. And besides, if people can't laugh at themselves, well I think they're stuffy old poops."

"But those supposed-funny-jokes are so EXAGGERATED."

"Of course they're exaggerated. That's the point of most humor. You can't tell about people's daily lives verbatim, it would be too dull. Heavenly-days, can you imagine anything duller than a bunch of Norwegians? Watching paint dry would be more exciting. That's why stories have to pick out the high lights—and the low lights—and add exaggeration. Which reminds me, did you hear about Sven Swedberg? He thinks 'Mass Transit' means a way to get Catholics to church. Ya-hoo! I'm on a roll with that one."

"You're on the down-hill roll again and showing the dark side of personality. It's really disgraceful. Genuine ethnic humor comes out of a group's unique culture and situations, events which enlighten and build empathy for the group while it amuses at the same time."

"Explain those fancy words, and enlighten me at the same time. Better yet, tell me a true ethnic-humor joke."

"Well, if you insist, here's one. Maybe. Anyway, it's a true story. This immigrant wrote an America-letter back to Norway, but he had learned a little English by then and his letter ended up being a combination of two languages. In the letter he stated: 'My barn burned, but I don't care that much. In America the barn can easily be replaced.' Well now, in Norway they thought the news in that letter was just horrible—and that Americans must be awful people—because the word 'barn' in Norwegian means children."

"Is that it? Are you done?"

"Yah, I mean yes."

"Is that all there was to it?"

"Yes. What did you think of it?"

"Now I think **that's** a dumb story. Worse than that, it's sick! Heck, I much prefer the story about this new insurance company started in Norway. It's called 'My Fault Insurance.'"

"Now there you go again. How do you expect to build pride in cultural ancestry with stories like that last one?"

"Pride? I've already got the pride. That comes before the jokes. I believe that any culture is at-ease with itself when they can tell stories about themselves. It's harmless and pointless but fun! Hey, when two Santa Clauses are up on the roof, how can you tell which one is Norwegian? "He's the one with the Easter basket. Wahoo!"

"Oh, brother, you're a lulu. That kind of story, I repeat, has no

redeeming virtue and works directly against the important goal
of building respect for divergent backgrounds."

"Ah, come off it. Erase those sixteen-cylinder words and all I
see is a thin-skinned guy who suffers mental bruises over alleged attacks on his beloved Scandinavians, attacks which
most people don't even see, let alone get disturbed about—let
alone get mad about. Heck, back in the Holy Land, in Norway,
they tell jokes about the Swedes. And vice versa in Sweden."

"Now hold it a minute. First, you're getting sacrilegious, and
secondly, I seem to have to remind you that mutual respect for
our differences in this country is the only basis for both
tolerance and the preservation of heritage."

"Now you hold your horses a moment. I'm all for respect and
preservation, but we can achieve both, regardless of ethnic
jokes. Hells-Bells, go to a Sons of Norway meeting and listen to
the stories they tell. They're all about Ole and Lars and Sven.
Now isn't that a good sign?"

"No, it's not. It's stupid. They're actually hurting themselves.
Scandinavian-Americans are not like that 'Ole-Lena' stuff any
more, and you know that's true."

"Okay, in part I agree—but just in part. Let me tell you about
this one man I know. He's much like you, except not so wordy.
Anyway, he was telling me—and this is the truth—and I got to
say it exactly the way he did. He said: 'Whenever I read heavy
Scandinavian dialect I get offended. Really angry. Iss that the
way we talk? No. By George, I wuss so mad when I saw that
one column. Fee-da.' That's just what he said and how he said
it."

"Even if Scandinavian s's carry over to the next generation,
I'm still with that man who abhors dialect-forms of humor. As
for anyone who still talks like that these days, well, all I can say
is. . . ."

"Uff da?"

"NO! No, not that disgusting phrase!"

"Well, it looks to me like we're getting nowhere fast. Our
problem may be like that of the Lutheran—"Lewtern"?—pastor
who loved Scandinavian ethnic jokes but was personally

Did you hear the one about the Norwegian who wore tinfoil on his nose? He was keeping his lunch warm.

bothered by any hint of insult. So he studied the Bible for help, looking for a people who no longer existed, believing he could use that extinct group as the butt of his stories, then no longer would he have to pick on the Norwegians. Anyway, he found such a group in the Bible, the Hittites. Oh, he was so pleased; now he had at least found somebody whose present ethnicity could not be tarnished nor insulted, and so he went to church the next Sunday and began his sermon with a story, as he usually did to get their attention. He said, 'Congregation, did you hear the story about the two Hittites? One was named Sven and the other named Ole. . . . ' "

(Silence. Long silence.) "Y'know, now I've got an appropriate story to tell **you**: What is black and blue and rolls in agony on the ground? Answer: YOU—if you tell another ethnic joke."

"Uff da."

The Weirdos Wandered At The Westly Place; Wot Dun It?

All the local citizens called it "The Westly Place." Well, not quite all; the old-timers called it "Da Vestly Pa-lace." Despite the farm not being owned by the Westly family for some twenty-five years, the name nevertheless hung on.

The Westly Place was a broken-down, fifty-acre farm about two miles out of town, and on this land there grew mainly rocks and sand-burrs, but its infamous reputation came not from the lousy land but from the weird assortment of humanity who occupied the land. The farm seemed to acquire more bizarre, immoral and just plain goofy families than all of the rest of the farms in the township combined.

The revolving number of renters over the years—and their squirrelly eccentricities—gave support to the prevailing viewpoint that this special plot of soil attracted the loony type of denizens who were only a half step away from either the 1) asylum, or 2) jail. (Several took that extra half step and made it to one or the other or both.)

The fact that the farm was always rented made it special in a negative sense. Almost all of the other farms in the region were family-owned, and family-operated, and thus the prevailing assumption among these owners was that while people in general who rented farms were suspect to start with, the people who rented the Westly Place were demented to start with.

Although the reasoning may seen unfair, the pattern of screw-ball-families who came to live on the Westly Place was so disgraceful as to mar with a foul reputation any newcomers who arrived to live there. New renters got immediate bad reputations in the community before they ever stepped outside the front door. Guilt by association; the farm contaminated all.

Indeed, the simple line "They live on the Westly Place" was sufficient explanation to typecast each new party who arrived at the homestead. And the poor kids who came to the school in town from that farm had two and nine-tenths strikes against them before they had a chance to open their mouths.

There was a common Norwegian one-line summary for the Westly Place inhabitants: **De er pakk** (they are trash), and the renters seemed to work extra hard to achieve this designation. For most of them it came so easy.

Then, of course, what the locals could not see and hear about the current family they would eventually make up, and these rumors bordered on the mind-boggling. Samples:

"Well, then, did you hear that the bunch there now is really part of a Gypsy group who plan to cast a spell on the livestock?"

"Well, then, I heard they're all a bunch of Communists! They've been sent here by the Russians to start a Commie cell in our community. After all, they eat borscht!"

"Well, then, they say that the last couple there weren't even married. They lived in sin! And they had three kids to show for it. Now our country has come to a fine fettle letting these loose women loose. And THAT MAN there said: 'Why pay for the cow when you can get the milk for free?' Uff da. Fee da. Shame!"

"Well, then, I hear they don't even eat potatoes. They eat rice! Can you ever imagine anyone so strange, then?"

The rumors were, naturally, more interesting than the facts, but there were plenty of facts, too, to keep the tag of riff-raff applicable. The obvious question for some townfolk was: What made the Westly Place people so strange in the first place? Was it the iron in the water? Was it the trolls allegedly hiding under the bridge on the long driveway to the farmhouse? Was it the contaminated 'stil-drippings they sipped on from the dirty copper-tubing pipes hidden in the haymow? Nope, none of these. The obvious answer for most people was simple: Welfare!

Being on the public dole, that's what ruined 'em! Or so said the consensus-report of the Mainstreet Mafia, the Hardware-Store-Hitmen who sat around all day gabbing and grousing, all the time making pious pronouncements on all things above and below the stratosphere, in this world and the next.

It was true that the Westly Place was the one and only spot in the township where the county welfare-agent made his regular stop, and this fact alone was sufficient documentary evidence to convict the whole kit-and-kaboodle of them as third class citizens, or so proclaimed the Gubrandsdal Godfather who weighed the shingle-nails and sold the horse-collars at the hardware store. He was happy to see every family leave; "good riddance of bad rubbish," was his summary; **De er pakk.**

And who were some the these Westly Place wastrels?

Well, there was the Tostenrud clan who lasted a year and a half. They slipped out the day before the sheriff arrived with a warrant for the husband's arrest. Although Mr. Tostenrud was barely literate, his penmanship capabilities were more than adequate for him to write a voluminous number of bad checks. But, like a bad fog at night that is gone by mid-morning, the Tostenruds just seemed to disappear into the morning sun Here today, gone tomorrow. Poof!

The Avelsgaard outfit, which lasted a whole two years before their eviction, were later to come to public attention as they managed to produce two boys who eventually matriculated all the way through the state penal system. Graduating from the county jail, the boys moved onward and upward to the state

"The farm seemed to acquire more bizarre, immoral and just plain goofy families than all of the rest of the farms in the township combined."

reformatory, and finally, in a burst of effort and energy (grand larceny and assault), they made it all the way to the state Big-House, Gray-Stone Tech. Alas, they fell just short of achieving federal status, however, never quite enrolling at Ft. Leavenworth. And the boys' mother too shall long be remembered in town for her once-uttered line at the corner tavern: "Aaaaah, den, but ay iss so prrrroud of my boyss, den."

A couple of the Westly Place gentry were to distinguish themselves as school janitors. Well, not really as janitors so much but for their going on long toots when they were supposed to be janitoring. One sweeper managed to stay drunk for five straight weeks, a distinguishing achievement indeed. Not only could he go better than a month without drawing a sober breath, he also could contribute a memorable line to the community's Hall of Fame for One-Liners. The hallowed literary sentence came when the local pastor asked the man what it would take to bring him back to full sobriety again, and the reply: "I'll need just one quart of Corby's whiskey to sober up on." And if that wasn't strange enough, the pastor actually did buy him a bottle and the man did drink it after which—some time after—he sobered up, dried out, cleaned up and went back to his short-lived job with the broom.

One Westly Place renter could barely talk, and when he did, he spoke a special language called Neanderthal. Few people ever heard him try to speak publicly, which was just as well, because what he allegedly said in each sentence combined obscenities, profanities and vulgarities. To illustrate (kind of) his elocution-pattern, he once looked at the grocery store owner and said: "Gimme sim nod-nam sip fer p'cikes."

"Huh?" replied the confused man behind the wooden counter.

The wife then interjected with the translation: "He wants syrup for pancakes."

As suggested, most ghetto inhabitants were pleased that the man's enunciation was as bad as it was. One of Igor's lamentations (the kids had named him Igor The Dinosaur) he would proclaim loudly and often on street corners relative to an admitted mistake he had made, namely raising chickens when he should have been producing cucumbers. It came out: "Futtin' chit-ens! Ness tim ay racin' tutumbersss!"

All in all the Westly Place outlaws were awful over the years; they gave the farm such a negative, disgraceful connotation to the point that had the Savior of the World appeared suddenly and announced to the locals that He would be spending some time with his disciples on the Westly Place, He, too, would have been disdained as a person and his ideas dismissed as devoid of serious consideration. After all, ***De er pakk,*** the whole lot of them.

Was it the iron in the water?. . .the trolls under the bridge?. . .

Everyone Addressed Him As 'Mister'

Just three months away from age 90, Mr. A. O. Lee died on June 17, 1983, at the Homme Nursing Home in Wittenberg, Wisconsin. Mr. Lee was a school-man almost all of his adult life; the last 30 school years he was Principal and Teacher of the Academy and the Union Free High School in Scandinavia, Wisconsin. Mr. Lee was my father.

The little boy begged his father to take him along again fishing, and the father honored the request once more, knowing it meant his doing everything for the child from baiting the hook to pulling in the blue-gills. Out on the lake, when the fish didn't bite immediately, the boy would want to go home right away, but the father always counseled patience: "Patience and endurance must be learned. Both are required for most good things in life." The father was right, of course.

Later, when the boy was about ten, the father would let him sit on his lap and steer their 1937 Plymouth while driving on nearly deserted country roads. The sight of another car caused the boy nearly to panic and he pleaded for advice on what to do!

"Stay calm, keep control," said the father, who then added: "But always drive like everybody else on the road is crazy." The father was right, of course. (That advice has always proved useful.)

The young lad of 14 came back home complaining about the Saturday morning confirmation lessons at the church: "Why we gotta learn this stuff? It's no fun." The father, who had quizzed his son on the memorization of Luther's **Small Catechism** prior to each Saturday session, informed the callow lad that all learning could not necessarily be fun nor should it be so: "Important information must be learned, regardless of how little 'fun' you believe it to be at the time." The father was right, of course. Some learning is hard but very important.

The headstrong, teen-age youth came home late at night, a half-hour after the time he had said he would return, and the father met him at the door with the news that the youth was hereby quarantined at home at night for a month, and his car privileges removed for the rest of the summer: "You made a promise, a contract, and you chose to break that agreement. It's that simple; you forfeited your rewards."

The father was right of course, as much as it hurt the grounded teenager at the time.

The father was right of course, as much as it hurt the grounded teenager at the time.

At the boy's high school he wondered how his teacher-principal-father could maintain such iron discipline, being that he was such a small man physically. All students were absolutely petrified of crossing this man. Just one strong glance of his eyes above the rims of his glasses would wither any adolescent. But when asked how he kept kids in line so easily, the father smiled and demured that he did not really know. But the son knew, of course, and the answer lay essentially in one word, respect.

This respect knew no age limit. The son was both amazed and amused that even most townspeople on Social Security always addressed his Dad as "Mr. Lee." An old-timer explained it to the confused son: "There are few people who deserve to be called Mister all their life, and he's one of them." The old-timer was right, of course. Together the old-timer and the son and the entire community had watched Mr. Lee give daily meaning to old but not old-fashioned words: patriotism, honor, integrity, duty, honesty, decency, courtesy. He didn't just talk about these words, he lived them.

Meanwhile, the high school senior son was uncertain about further education, but his father knew the answer clearly: "An education is something that cannot be taken away from anyone. You may have many regrets in later life, but getting college degrees will never be one of them." The father was right, of course.

The son went on to become a social studies school teacher like his father, and later they had a discussion on proper teaching attire. In an era of casualness, when most men teachers began showing up at school in sport coats and sport shirts, in cords and T-shirts, and worse, the father still wore a suit and a tie and shined shoes each day, every day. No exceptions His explanation was simple: "Whether it's a concert or a classroom, it's 'First through the eyes, then through the ears.' And besides, students deserve the best. Remember, schools are for the students, not for the teachers." The father was right, of course.

Retirement at age 65 was a mixed blessing for the father. He missed the students and the classroom; however, he did not miss the administrative duties. Advancing years had the advantage of freedom from assignments, but they also served as a reminder of mortality.

"Growing old is not for cowards," he advised. He was right, of course.

"Growing old is not for cowards," he advised. He was right, of course.

Even in his 80's, the father's habits did not change much. he placed the American flag outside in its stand every single morning at sun-up; Bible-reading and devotions followed. After breakfast, magazines were devoured, books were pored over, three daily newspapers were consumed, and, later, television-news and documentaries were watched with eager fascination. The mind stayed as sharp as ever. Moreover, the garden produced mightily; brook trout filled the freezer; and one brandy-on-ice preceded each supper.

And yet, finally, the father began slowing down: the gardens got smaller, then were abandoned; the fishing trailed off, finally for good; the reading diminished in quantity, then quality; the t-v was turned off for good; the brandy went untouched.

Upon entering the nursing home in the Fall of '82, the father declined quickly, after Christmas. The father became, at times, confused and disoriented, but only at times. He was slipping. He knew it. He knew that he sometimes knew not, and this knowledge bothered him immensely.

The son, now middle-aged himself, came to visit him and the father did not know the son at first. In his wheel-chair the father was unsure of his present whereabouts, but he spoke with clarity of his childhood days on his emigrant father's farm in Iowa; with total recall he told of the pioneer, primitive life he lived as a young boy—and how yet it was all so wonderful; then he described chilling scenes of his World War I experiences in the trenches of northern France, of crawling in mud under the barbed-wire in no-man's-land, of going without food for two days. Then before long the father's mind came back again to the present, and he was fully lucid when he commented on his own failing condition of that moment: "Sometimes we live too long."

Perhaps he was right, of course; he was always right before. Whatever the accuracy, the father, the teacher, the civic servant —Mr. Lee—is gone now. Those many persons who knew him, whose lives were touched if not altered by his truly honorable person, have had their own lives diminished by his absence, but they are nevertheless rewarded by the legacy of his memory. After all, the "Mr. Lees" of this world don't come along very often in a lifetime.

Addendum:

After the funeral was over, I sought out this one man in particular to give special thanks to him because the man had given up a day of work, a day's wages, to be a pallbearer. This person had been a former student of Mr. Lee's and in later years he was also his neighbor. I went to thank him for any extra trouble that this funeral might have caused him. "Trouble?" he replied, unbelievingly. "It was no trouble at all. It was a real honor to be asked to be a pallbearer for Mr. Lee. In fact, it shall rank as one of the greatest honors of my life."

A.O. Lee used to tell his classes, somewhat facetiously, that the mark of success for any person would be revealed at that person's funeral. As it turned out, the pallbearer's comment reveals that Mr. Lee was right again, of course.

Final Epilogue

Some readers of the above tribute to my late father may perceive the comments as pleasant enough, yet little more than a few appropriate lines of respect from a dutiful son for a decent Dad. But it is more than that because he was more than that. As a semi-public figure, he effected and affected the lives of hundreds of persons. The letters and cards pouring in following his funeral attest to his specialness.

Wrote one older lady, a former student of his: "Of all the people in the world whom I have personally known over many years, A.O. Lee was the only person who never changed, who never wore thin; he was a life-long role model."

Perhaps the most articulate of the comments received came in a letter from another former student who is now a dean and a professor of English at the University of Nebraska. He wrote:

"To a boy growing up in Scandinavia, he was both a model and a source of pride. As I, too, pass into middle age, I've found that few of my mentors stand up very well against the test of time. In recent years I've discovered that A.O. Lee and what he stood for mean more to me now than ever, and I've found myself thinking about him and those days in Scandinavia. He knew what education was all about—that long after the Latin verbs were forgotten and the dates of history faded into obscurity, what would live on in his students was the example of a good man, who lived his life with integrity and selflessness, serving his family and community. I am grateful every day that A.O. Lee was part of my life."

The last time I saw my father alive was two weeks prior to his death. We visited together in his nursing-home room, he seated in a wheelchair and I on his bed. By then he had lost considerable weight and understandably did not look at all the way I had always known and remembered him. His once-piercing blue eyes had sort of filmed over, the deep blue paling with the rheumy-look associated with the aged.

But his voice was still strong and he tried to speak with that same brusqueness and command that was always so much a part of him. Even in a wheelchair he still had presence. He then wanted to talk about the same three topics he had enjoyed discussing a lifetime: the news of the world, the stock market, and American history. He began by questioning the wisdom of recent presidential and congressional decisions and easily made quick historical allusions to similar circumstances in the past. He was enjoying himself.

Those three topics were subject matter he truly loved discussing. He had always thrived on hard information and was suspicious of anything that smacked of sentimentality. He hated novels, for example. Hence he never was one for making personal commendations, was terribly tight with compliments, and a bit short on humor. In brief, he seemed to be a stereotypical Norwegian-American—unattached, uninvolved, unemotional, fitting the description of the cold Norwegian husband who loved his wife so much that he almost told her so. Besides always keeping his emotional distance, he had a touch of fatalistic Norwegian pessimism: if the sun is shining brightly today, well, we'll pay for it tomorrow.

As our conversation continued, it was clear that he was getting tired, both from thinking about the state of the world (not good) as well as physically talking about it at length. To try to change the topic and brighten things up, I stated with mock forcefulness a line that his emigrant father had said so often: "Vi har det godt i Amerika" (We have it good in America). To these words he smiled broadly, then nodded, then said, "That's right. He was right, you know; despite our complaining he was right," and he seemed to be thinking about that statement as he kept nodding his head in assent.

It was now time to leave. I got up to shake his hand and we would say our formal goodbyes the same cold, proper way we had said them to each other for two generations. This procedure was again carried out and I stood in the doorway to leave. It was then that he turned in his chair, gently grabbed my forearm and said what were to be his last words to me, words I shall never forget and shall forever cherish: "By the way, I'm sure proud of you, son. And these days there isn't much to be proud about."

A few seconds later I stood alone in the corridor. At that moment I could not see, or talk, and I could hardly stand; I had to lean on the wall for support. It took a full five minutes to compose myself enough that I could walk away from my father's room.

In a half century I have been reasonably fortunate. I have achieved some awards and rewards. But no reward shall ever be bigger than those few simple words spoken to me by a ninety-year old man.

Yes, Vi har det godt i Amerika.

The End

A. O. Lee (1893-1983) Picture taken circa 1950

"Everyone Addressed Him As 'Mister.' " (story in last section, p. 209)

MR. AND MRS. A.O. LEE. Picture taken in the summer of 1982 and their last picture taken together. Mr. Lee (Arthur) died in June, 1983; Mrs. Lee (Arla), age 89 at this writing, lives in the Homme Home For the Aged in Wittenberg, Wisconsin. A.O. and Arla Lee had four children: (in order of birth) Sylvia Madelyn, Loren James, Robert Edward, and Arthur Ophelius, Jr., the author of this book. Madelyn (Mrs. Arne Larson) had been a school librarian in Appleton, Wisconsin; she passed away from cancer a month before her father died; she was 62. Loren is a real estate broker in Northfield, Minnesota. Robert is the Director of Bands at Wartburg College, Waverly, Iowa. Art is a professor of history at Bemidji State University, Minnesota.

Arla Scarvie Lee

"She had those special, gentle hands. . ." (story on p. 167)
(see also *The Lutefisk Ghetto*, p. 183)

Scandinavia Lutheran Church

"The long-awaited event was almost here—the annual
Church Lutefisk Supper." (story on p. 86)

Formal Lee Family Photo

Coming home on furlough during World War II (Loren in uniform) was a time for many families to take official portraits. (for war-time story, see p. 127)

"Bucky and Gordon"

"Gordon looked suspiciously at the squad's favorite player and character, the portly Bucky Carr." (see stories on pp. 37 and 83)

The Lee Family (circa 1937)
at "the farm" in Decorah, Iowa

"It was a journey dreaded by our entire family, and we made that trip each year." (story on p. 47)

The Grade School

"We believed we were rather sophisticated because we attended a 'city school' that had four rooms." (story on p. 72)

The Lee Family Home

"Their home a large, 10-room, red-brick, two-story house with creaky wooden floors that tilted and sagged, and it had a balky, lump-coal fired furnace that sometimes worked." (story in *The Lutefisk Ghetto,*, p. 183)

Academy/Union Free High School

"The school was the lengthened shadow of that man. He was a life-long role model." (see Epilogue, p. 213)

Scandinavia Co-op

"Big robbery in town. Seems these two guys were trying to siphon gas from a truck down by the Co-op." (story in *The Lutefisk Ghetto,* p. 154)

The Fairgrounds and Ball Park

"Time was when summer Sunday afternoon baseball was the biggest thing around." (story on p. 37)